The Essence

(A Collection of Short Stories from the
Ancient Scripture of India: Shrimad
Bhagavatam)

1

Sunil Das. K.

DEDICATION

"Whatever I have achieved and whatever I wish to achieve, I am not the doer of these. O Madhusudan, you are the real doer, and you alone are the enjoyer of their results."

This book is dedicated to my parents, my wife Sasmita, my son Om, and my cherished daughter Komal. This book is also dedicated to each one of my family members, friends, pupils, and readers worldwide. I am grateful for everything you have given to my life.

Even though I am fully aware of how little I know about Lord Krishna and his teachings, I tried to write this series of books out of a strong desire to impart Lord Krishna's wisdom to my loved ones, friends, students, and readers.
Dedicated to my dear Lord Krishna, who means the world to me.
Hare Krishna!

CONTENTS

Acknowledgments

I am indebted to, his grace Gaura Chandra Prabhu and Binapani Mataji of Calgary, Canada for their fervent dedication to spiritual advancements and their immense love for Krishna and the Lord Jagannatha, which undoubtedly inspired me. I owe you for the hours we spent discussing the topics from Shrimad Bhagavatam and Bhagavat Gita.

I am also appreciative of Srila Prabhupada, the founder Acharya of ISKCON, and all his writings, lectures, publications, devotion, and teachings. I sincerely appreciate and thank all the devotees of Lord Krishna and adherents for their lectures, films, and interviews that are posted on online platforms.

During this project as well as others that were linked, I had the pleasure of working with each of the previously mentioned individuals has given me a great deal of professional and personal advice and has taught me a lot about life in general and scientific study.

Background:

The Supreme Lord first revealed this fundamental truth of the Bhagavatam to Brahma. It was given to Krishna Dwaipayan Vyasa by Brahma, who then passed it on to the great sage Narada Muni (Vyasadeva). Additionally, Vyasa dictated the Shrimad-Bhagavatam to Shukadeva Goswami, who then read it to Maharaja Parikshit.

The story of how the narration between Sukadeva Goswami and King Parikshit took place demonstrates the significance of both the Bhagavatam and the sacred site of Shukratal. King Parikshit is the grandson of the legendary warrior Arjuna and the son of Abhimanyu. He was about 60 years old when he stumbled upon Shamik the Sage's hermitage while searching for water. He disrespected Shamik, a sage who was in deep meditation and unaware of the King's presence, because of his mischief or pride. The young son of the sage Shamik, Shringi, became enraged with King Parikshit after learning about the incident with his father. After that, Shringi cursed the

King, saying that he would perish in seven days.

The King, who saw his predicament as a blessing, gave his kingdom to his son Janamejay and went to the Ganges to fast for the seven days leading up to his snake bite. The King, who saw his predicament as a blessing, gave his kingdom to his son Janamejay and went to the Ganges to fast for the seven days leading up to his snake bite. He saw a group of holy men gathered nearby. "O great sages, what is the most crucial duty of one who is about to die?" the King then questioned them.

Shukadeva, the great sage and 16-year-old son of Vyasadeva, was ambling nearby, carefree and content with himself. He was being followed by kids while dressed in the avadhuta (spiritually entranced aesthetic) garb and acting neglected by others. Additionally, King Parikshit asked Shukadeva a question: "Since you are the greatest of saints, what should a man do when he is about to die?" What is it that he should chant, hear, remember, and worship?

In his initial response, Shukadeva said, "The question

you have posed is glorious because it is helpful to everyone. All transcendentalists agree that the answer to this query is the fundamental theme of life. One should have the courage to face death head-on when they are nearing the end of their lives. But one must give up any attachment to the physical body, as well as any desires related to it.

Sage Sukadeva Goswami starts narrating the glory of Lord Krishna and his pastimes, the events, and his teachings to Maharaja Parikshit.

Introduction:

The saying "Education is Life and Life is an Education" has always been a personal motto of mine. We learn as we mature, with significant assistance from our parents, teachers, mentors, the government, and society. But we only have so much time in this world to discover, reflect, go back, fix, and accomplish everything.

All ages are encouraged to read this book, but young people with a busy future are the target audience. Anything new can be started at any time. I hope this compilation will be enjoyable for my readers.

India's ancient writings have undergone several revisions, rewrites, revisions, and verification. Even today, there are numerous manuscripts of this type, such as the Puranas and Samhitas, that tell the tales of India's ancient history and civilization.

This book is a collection of tales drawn from reliable religious texts like the Mahabharata, the Ramayana, the Bhagwat Gita, and the Shrimad Bhagavatam.

Shrimad Bhagavatam's essence is the same as the essence of everything. All the Vedas, all of philosophy, all of knowledge, all of theology, all of religion, and all of action are based on it. This can be shown, so it is not exaggeration.

The 18,000 verses of the exquisite poem Shrimad Bhagavatam, which was uttered and recorded 5000 years ago, do not contain the word "Hindu" or "Hinduism" even once. This exquisite poem refers to an atom as "anu" and describes it as the fundamental unit of matter before moving on to higher units of measurement that elegantly combine space and time, as well as defining time in terms of matter and vice versa.

It is significant to note at this point that Shrimad Bhagavatam (12.2.1) describes modern life appropriately. It states that at the start of the Kali Yuga (current millennium), individuals will have short lifespans, make large housing debts, and work all their lives in slavery to pay back the loans. They will not possess the intelligence to consider their own spiritual development. People will lose their sense of purpose and become lethargic and uninformed of what true happiness is. Because of the strong impact of the Kali Yuga, religion, honesty, cleanliness, tolerance, mercy, longevity, physical strength, and memory would all deteriorate with time. Men no longer defend their aging parents.

Men will grow angry with one another in the Kali Yuga even over a few pennies. They will be willing to slaughter even their own relatives and give up all cordial relationships.

A verse (SB12.03.51) says, "My dear King, although Kali-yuga is an ocean of faults, there is still one good quality about this age: Simply by chanting the Hare Krishna Maha-mantra, one can become free from material bondage and be promoted to the transcendental kingdom," is included in addition to all the depressing facts above. People can be freed from all bonds and from the bonds of this materialism just by uttering the name of Hari. Since I lack the credentials and knowledge to talk about the Bhagavatam, I shall instead attempt to mention numerous smart and experienced experts.

"O best of the Brahmanas, the meaning of the Puranas is unchanging just like that of the Vedas," the Skanda Purana's Prabhasa-khanda (5.3.121–124) declares. There is no doubt that the Puranas contain all the Vedas. The Veda worries that individuals who are not qualified to understand it may misinterpret it. The Puranas and Itihasas thereby established the Vedic relevance. The Smriti contains information that is absent from the Vedas. The Puranas provide information that is absent from the Smriti.

Those who are knowledgeable about the Vedas and Upanishads but not the Puranas are not considered learned. Like how Gitopanisad contains the essence of all Upanishads, Bhagavat Purana contains the essence of all Puranas.

The Garuda Purana is quoted by Madhavacharya in his book Bhagavata-Tatparya. This [Purana] is all finished. It establishes the meaning of the Mahabharata, provides a commentary on Gayatri, and concludes the message of the Vedas. It is the purport of the Vedanta sutra. The Sama Veda is one of the Puranas, and it was recited by the god Vyasa himself.

Shrimad-Bhagavatam is the name of this work, which has twelve cantos, hundreds of chapters, and eighteen thousand verses.

Numerous more lines extol the Bhagavata as superior to all other Puranas. These include to name a few, the Vishnu Khanda of the Skanda Purana (5.16.40, 42, 44, 33), the Matsya Purana (53.20-22), the Agni Purana (272.6.7), and the Padma Purana (Uttara-khanda 193.3).

Sri Krishna's feet are represented by the Bhagavatam's first and second cantos. His thighs are the third and fourth cantos. His navel is the fifth canto. It is His chest in the sixth canto. His arms are the seventh and eighth cantos. His throat is the ninth canto. His lovely lotus face is described in the ninth canto. His forehead appears in the eleventh canto. He is the focus of the twelfth canto. I prostrate before the Lord, the ocean of mercy, who emerges in this scene with skin the color of a tamala tree. The essence of Bhagavatam is contained in these four verses.

1.   Brahma, it is I, the Personality of Godhead,

who was existing before the creation, when there was nothing but Myself. Nor was there the material nature, the cause of this creation. That which you see now is also I, the Personality of Godhead, and after annihilation what remains will also be I, the Personality of Godhead. SB 2.9.33

2. O Brahma, whatever appears to be of any value, if it is without relation to Me, has no reality. Know it as My illusory energy, that reflection which appears to be in darkness. SB 2.9.34

3. O Brahma, please know that the universal elements enter the cosmos and at the same time do not enter the cosmos; similarly, I also exist within everything created, and at the same time I am outside of everything. SB 2.9.35

4. A person who is searching after the Supreme Absolute Truth, the Personality of Godhead, must certainly search for it up to this, in all circumstances, in all space and time, and both directly and indirectly. SB 2.9.36

These verses are the subject of volumes of literature, interpretations, and comments that are now available. It is utterly difficult for me to write about this divine wisdom given my minuscule understanding of it.

The most important thing is to adhere to religious rules, and the most important rule is to serve the Supreme Lord with pure devotion by singing His holy name. Hare Krishna. The highest form of religion for every living thing in human civilization is devotional worship, which begins with reciting the Lord's holy name. SB 6.3.22

The sole intention to provide these stories is to give a starting point of devotion and living life happily while getting directions and finding the solutions to today's chaotic, confusing, and, problematic situations we go through in our day-to-day lives. We are all busy in our lives, many questions come to our mind when we are in a delicate situation. Such as, what is the solution? where is the solution? where it came from? what are my initiatives? Am I destined to have to face these situations? and tons of similar questions. Our bewildered mind is always busy with day-to-day life chores and so-called entertainment. We have health issues, relationship issues, financial issues, and so on. As human beings, it is very difficult to manage all these things to our benefit of ourselves.

This book contains 36 short stories, it will allow the reader to learn, pause and review the situations and find solutions through the stories. It is a collection of short stories from the ancient Indian scriptures primarily Shrimad Bhagavatam. This book is solely dedicated to my dear lord Krishna,

Hare Krishna!

What is the Right Path to Devotion?

Uddhava's responses to Lord Krishna. Uddhava was a close companion of Lord Shri Krishna and is considered to be one of the best thinkers (Brahma Gyani) during the Dwapar era. "O Krishna!" he once cried out to Shri Krishna. Numerous spiritualists are promoting various routes. Please give your recommendations on the right and wrong paths. Why so many different routes? The various routes appear to be at odds with one another. Because they lack knowledge, people become perplexed when they learn about all these alternative paths and are unable to choose the best one to choose. Please help me to sort this out. A blind person cannot make decisions involving sight.

In the Kaliyuga, numerous new religions will blossom, according to Uddhava. So, to get an answer straight from Lord Krishna before the Kaliyuga began, he asked Him this inquiry. The notion is that no one can oppose the correct path to reach the Lord once He confirms it personally. Noting that Uddhava was a brilliant Gyani, it should be noted that he already knew the answer to the question he posed. He only posed the query for us to read it, take something away from it, and go in the proper direction.

Shrimad Bhagavad Mahapuran Uddhava contains Lord Krishna's response to this query. I made known the different methods for achieving My fulfillment in the Vedas. I gave the Vedas to the creator Brahma before the creation. The same information was delivered by Brahma to his son Manu and other holy people. Then it was revealed to Bhrigu and from him to Saptarishis, who in turn passed it on to their sons.

These rules therefore reached the Gandharvas, demons, celestial Gods, and humans. Vedic texts were studied and pondered by people who had innately diverse mental traits. Over the course of their numerous prior lives, they had amassed several sankaras. Additionally, their attitudes and interests were dissimilar. As a result, those with sattvik temperament interpreted the Vedas in a sattivik way, people with rajasik temperament did the same, and people with tamasik temperament did the same.

Multiple routes emerged as a result.

Some routes developed because of traditions; for instance, an ancestor may have begun a ceremony of his own design, and many centuries later, people continue to blindly practice it.

Hypocrites built some roads to serve their own interests. People in the Kaliyuga invented the idea of false gods, for their personal gain. Some people are adamant about following the yagna and anushthaan (Vedic injunctions) and tapa (austerities) rules. Some people placed a strong emphasis on generosity (daan), while others stressed truthfulness, fasting, self-controlling of the senses, and so on. Then there are those who contend that gratifying one's own desires is the best course of action. To "eat, drink, and be merry" one should not worry about the afterlife.

The Lord declared, "Uddhava! These approaches do not lead to long-lasting outcomes. All of them result in fleeting happiness that is illusory, which plunges one into total sorrow.

Therefore, Uddhava, all of these and any new ones

that will be created are abhorrent. The only way to Me, the indescribable ocean of ecstasy, is via selfless bhakti, or devotion. According to the Vedas, anyone can practice bhakti in all circumstances, everywhere, always, with all senses engaged, without engaging any senses, with all material objects present, and without any object. Bhakti may provide anyone is wants because it is the mother of wisdom and renunciation. It cleanses one of past wrongdoings, eliminates the desire to sin in the present, and continues to bring joy.

Even though God is unbeatable, bhakti makes the Supreme Lord a slave. The Supreme Lord Shri Krishna remarked to the Gopis (milkmaids who lived in Vraj), "Since you forsook the world for My sake, I will remain indebted to you forever." Those who practice unwavering devotion (bhakti) to the Supreme Lord and have no selfish desires imprison Him with their adoration. And they are served by the Supreme Lord. Therefore, serving God in humility is the one and only true religion. All other methods are useless.

The devotion and service of the devotees of Lord

Vishnu are like the nourishing sap that flows through the tree, sustaining all its parts. The selfless actions of these devotees, who are guided by the teachings of the Bhagavat Gita and other sacred texts, inspire others to follow in their footsteps and work towards a more peaceful and harmonious world. Through their example, they demonstrate that true happiness and fulfillment can only be found in serving a higher purpose, beyond one's own selfish desires. May we all strive to emulate the devotion and selflessness of these great souls, and in doing so, contribute to a more enlightened and compassionate society.

Lord Krishna - Karna Conversation

The strong warrior Karna, a great devotee of Lord Krishna, asks Lord Krishna in a Bhakta-Bhagavan discussion,

"My mother deserted me the instant I was born. I was born an illegitimate child; is it my fault?

Because I was not regarded as a Kshatriya, Guru Dhronacharya did not provide me with an education. After teaching me, Guru Parashuraam cursed me with forgetfulness after learning that I was the son of Kunti and a Kshatriya.

My arrow accidentally hit a cow, and the cow's owner cursed me for no reason of my own.

In Draupadi's Swayamvar, I suffered a scandal.

Even Kunti Mata admitted the truth to me at last, but only to protect her other sons.
Whatever I received was through Duryodhana's charity. So how am I wrong in taking his side ???"

I was born in a prison, Lord Krishna responds to Karna. Before I was even born, death was already waiting for me. I was separated from my birth parents the night I was born.

You were exposed to the sounds of swords, chariots, horses, bows, and arrows from an early age. Even before I could walk, all I encountered were a cow herd's shed, excrement, and numerous attempts on my life.

Without the Army, there is no education. People were blaming me for all their issues, I could hear blaming me for everything. I had not even started my studies when your teachers were praising you all for your bravery. I did not enroll in Rishi Sandipani's Gurukul till I was 16 years old.

To protect them from Jarasandh, I had to relocate my entire tribe from the Yamuna's banks, which were dangerously close to the ocean. I was criticized for fleeing and labelled a coward!

You will be given a lot of credit if Duryodhana wins the war. If Dharmaraja wins the battle, what do I get?

The war and all associated issues are solely to blame...

Karna, keep this in mind. Everybody must overcome obstacles in life. Nobody has it easy or fair in life! But your mind (conscience) is aware of what is Right (Dharma). It does not matter how many injustices we experienced, how many times we were embarrassed, or how many times we fell—what matters is how you responded at the time.

The unfairness of life does not give us permission to make poor decisions. We must always keep in mind that while life may be challenging at times, our fate is not determined by the shoes we wear but rather by the actions we take.

It is up to us to choose our path and take responsibility for our choices. We must strive to do what is right, even when it is difficult. Our conscience will guide us toward the right decisions, and we must trust in its wisdom. It is important to remember that we are not defined by our past mistakes or misfortunes. Instead, we should use them as opportunities for growth and learning.

Life may not always be fair, but we have the power to make it better by choosing to live with integrity and compassion. Let us embrace the challenges that come our way and use them as opportunities to become stronger, wiser, and more resilient individuals.

As Mata Kunti spoke to Lord Krishna, Shrimad Bhagavatam, 1.8.25

"I wish that all those calamities would happen again and again so that we could see You again and again, for seeing You means that we will no longer see repeated births and deaths."

Also, The Ramayana teaches us that even though we may face challenges and obstacles in life, we must trust the process and have faith in the grand coordinator.

This world is temporary and often presents a false reality, but by remaining devoted to God, we can find everlasting peace and fulfillment. Just like flowers blossoming on trees sessional, our blessings may not always be visible in the present moment, but we must wait for the next season and trust that everything will fall into place. As we navigate through life's ups and downs, let us remember to keep our faith strong and our hearts open to the divine guidance that surrounds us. With patience and perseverance, we can overcome any obstacle and find true happiness in this world.

Shrimad Bhagavatam for the West

People from diverse religious and cultural backgrounds, those who have never been exposed to India or ancient Indian theology and philosophy, or those who are Westerners may question the adequacy of reading, learning, and understanding Shrimad Bhagavatam.

Although at first it could be difficult for someone who has never encountered India, its faith and culture. It is nothing new; it is only the way of life from a different perspective, so with time it will become more comfortable. explained using examples from discussions, situations, and characters.

However, it is important to note that Shrimad Bhagavatam is not just a religious text, but a philosophical masterpiece that delves into the fundamental questions of existence and the nature of reality. Its teachings are universal and can be applied to any individual regardless of their background or beliefs. The text emphasizes the importance of self-realization and the cultivation of spiritual knowledge, which can lead to a deeper understanding of oneself and the world around us. Through its stories and teachings, Shrimad Bhagavatam offers a unique perspective on life that can inspire individuals to live with greater purpose and meaning. Therefore, even those who are unfamiliar with Indian culture or religion can benefit from reading and studying this profound work.

Shrimad Bhagavatam is a mass of stories that are sometimes incomprehensible to a person brought up today believing in modern science or Biblical traditions. The stories illustrate philosophical points untouched by Western philosophy.

It has a natural commentary on the Vedanta sutra and is the most lofty and conclusive of all scriptures. The literary incarnation of Lord Krishna, it is the most accurate and comprehensive portrayal of the Unchangeable Truth. According to scholars, it is the repository of the most secret information, the ultimate authority on every subject, and the richest source of devotion.

Is the core of all Vedic literature, the crowning achievement of the Vedas, the rulebook for human civilization, the foundation for self-realization, the wellspring of freedom, the pinnacle of all knowledge, and the most complete and authoritative text on yoga. It is the greatest blessing, the most delightful experience, the remover of all material unhappiness, and most importantly, the greatest source of wisdom and devotion for all living things.

Because they have implicit faith in it, thousands of people outside of India hold Shrimad Bhagavatam with the highest regard and veneration. Few Western academics and scholars may be aware of Shrimad Bhagavatam's importance among the Puranas, but unless they actively practice what they preach, they may not accept Shrimad Bhagavatam's nectar.

Sometimes, to understand the Bhagavatam, you must reject practically everything you were taught as a child to be true. It has been around for more than 150 trillion years. A huge form of God that is lying on a snake floating in the water revealed the secondary creator of the universe as a lotus flower emerging from the navel of the being. Each world weighs no more than a mustard seed to Him, and the others are on the hood of another enormous snake. God can take the shape of a fish, a boar, a tortoise, a man-lion hybrid, a dwarf, etc. In addition to parents and a sibling, God also has girlfriends. Indra removes the wings of the soaring mountains.… A praying elephant offered lovely philosophic prayers. God rides an enormous eagle-like creature to travel the universe. A demon became so powerful he controlled the seasons…. Prajapati creates all the species from their own bodies… many such things you may come across which does not align with science, confusion about timelines, etc.

Where do you start?

You must begin with the conviction that there is another perspective on things, one based on extremely ancient, revealed wisdom. The founder of ISKCON, Srila Prabhupada, had a profound comprehension of the Bhagavatam and God and lived humbly and devotedly as His servant. He rendered numerous spiritual texts into English. His physical presence and his teachings had a profound impact on thousands of people's lives, and they still have an impact today despite his physical absence. His insights are profound, and he has shown his love for God by remaining steadfast in his devotion to serving Him and making connections to Him as simple and effective as possible in the face of adversity and disappointments.

Shrimad Bhagavatam teaches us to live life with no desire to cheat, but to help; no desire to mislead, but to correct; and no desire for gain, but a desire to give freely. It is the most sublime, profound, informative, and perfect embodiment of all Vedic literature.

This Bhagavata Purana presents the utmost truth, which is understandable by those devotees who are entirely pure in heart, while categorically rejecting any religious actions which are motivated by material interests. Realities that are differentiated from illusions for the benefit of everyone are the highest truths. The triple miseries are uprooted by such reality.

The Supreme Lord is established in one's heart as soon as one listen to the Bhagavatam message with attention and submission, according to this culture of knowledge. SB 1.1.2

If you are familiar with Gita then dive into Shrimad Bhagavatam and enjoy the ocean of nectar. In verse SB 1.1.3, it is mentioned.

Enjoy Shrimad-Bhagavatam, the ripe fruit of the Vedic literary desire tree, o wise and knowledgeable humankind. It came from Sri Sukadeva Goswami's mouth. As a result, this fruit has acquired even more flavor; its nectar liquid was already palatable to everyone, including freed souls. It is chock-full of tales from God's history, among many other things, and LOVE, above all. The moment is now more than ever to give in to your urge to read and study Shrimad Bhagavatam.

Injustice to Pandavas

Wonderful Viveka explanation from Lord Krishna. Uddhava had been riding in Krishna's chariot and providing for him in a variety of ways since he was a little child. He did not ask Lord Krishna for any wishes or blessings. Dear Uddhava, throughout this incarnation of mine, many people have begged and received boons from me; nevertheless, you never asked me anything. When Lord Krishna was on the point of finishing His incarnation, and He is so kind, He called Uddhava. Do you not have any desire? I will be able to finish this avatar with the knowledge that I also helped you in some way.

Uddhava was an excellent gyani who had grown up watching Krishna. He had always been perplexed by what seemed to be a discrepancy in Krishna's teachings and deeds, and he wanted to know why. "Lord, you taught us to live in one way, but you lived in a different way," he questioned Krishna one day. I did not really comprehend many aspects of the Mahabharata drama, including your acts and the part you played. I am interested to know why you did what you did.

"Uddhava, what I told Arjuna during the Battle of Kurukshetra was from the Bhagavad Gita," Krishna remarked. My comments to you are now referred to as the "Uddhava Gita." I gave you this chance for that reason. Please do not be afraid to inquire.

Uddhava starts asking – 'Krishna, first tell me who is a real friend?' Krishna says, 'The real friend is one who comes to the help of his friend in need even without being called.'

Uddhava: 'Krishna, you were a dear friend of the Pandavas. They trusted you fully as Apadhbhandava (protector from all difficulties). Krishna, you not only know what is happening, but you know what is going to happen.

You are a great gyani. Just now you gave the definition of a true, close friend. Then, why your actions are not as per your definition? Why didn't you stop Dharmaraj (Yudhishthira) from gambling?

Ok, you may have a valid reason; Why did not you turn the luck in favor of Dharmaraj, by which you would have ensured that dharma wins?

You did not do that as well. At least you could have saved Dharmaraj by stopping the game after he lost his wealth, country, and himself. You could have released him from the punishment for gambling. Or, you could have entered the hall when he started betting on his brothers. You did not do that either.

Maybe when Duryodhana tempted Dharmaraj by offering to return everything lost if he betted Draupadi (who always brought good fortune to Pandavas), you could have intervened and with your divine power you could have made the dice roll in a way that is favorable to Dharmaraj.

Instead, you intervened only when Draupadi almost lost her modesty and now you claim that you gave clothes and saved Draupadi's modesty; how can you even claim this – after her being dragged into the hall by a man and disrobed in front of so many people.

What modesty is left for a woman? What have you

saved? How can you be called 'Apadhbhandava.'

If you cannot help in the time of crisis, what is the use? Is it Dharma?' As Uddhava posed these questions, tears started rolling from his eyes.

These are not the questions of Uddhava alone. All of us who have read Mahabharata have these questions. On behalf of us, Uddhava had already asked Krishna.

Lord Krishna, Swayam Bhagavan, smiled and said, 'Dear Uddhava, the law of this world is: 'only the one who has Viveka (intelligence through discrimination), wins. While Duryodhana had Viveka, Dharmaraj lacked it. That is why Dharmaraj lost.'

Uddhava was lost and confused. Krishna continues 'While Duryodhana had lots of money and wealth to gamble, he did not know how to play the game of dice. That is why he used his Uncle Shakuni to play the game while he betted. That is Viveka. Dharmaraj also could have thought similarly and offered that I, his cousin, would play on his behalf. If Shakuni and I had played the game of dice, who do you think would have won? Can he roll the numbers I am calling or would I roll the numbers he is asking?

Forget this. I can forgive the fact that he forgot to include me in the game. But, without Viveka, he did another blunder.

He prayed that I should not come to the hall as he did not want me to know that through ill fate, he was compelled to play this game. He tied me with his prayers and did not allow me to get into the hall; I was just outside the hall waiting for someone to call me through their prayers.

Even when Bheema, Arjuna, Nakula, and Sahadeva were lost, they were only cursing Duryodhana and brooding over their fate; they forgot to call me.

Even Draupadi did not call me when Dusshasan held her hair and dragged her to fulfill his brother's order. She was also arguing in the hall, based on her own abilities. She never called me.

Finally, good sense prevailed; when Dusshasan started disrobing her, she gave up depending on her own strength, and started shouting 'Hari, Hari, Abhayam

Krishna, Abhayam' and shouted for me. Only then I got an opportunity to save her modesty. I reached as soon as I was called. I saved her modesty. What is my mistake in this situation?

'Wonderful explanation, Kahna, I am impressed. However, I am not deceived. Can I ask you another question,' says Uddhava. Krishna gives him the permission to proceed.

'Does it mean that you will come only when you are called! Will you not come on your own to help people in crisis, to establish justice?' asks Uddhava.

Krishna smiles. 'Uddhava, in this life everyone's life proceeds based on their own karma. I do not run it; I do not interfere in it. I am only a 'witness.' I stand close to you and keep observing whatever is happening. This is God's Dharma.'

'Wow, very good Krishna. In that case, you will stand close to us, observe all our evil acts; as we keep committing more and more sins, you will keep watching us. You want us to commit more blunders, accumulate sins and suffer,' says Uddhava.

Krishna says. 'Uddhava, please realize the deeper meaning of your statements. When you understand & realize that I am standing as witness next to you, how could you do anything wrong or bad. You cannot do anything bad. You forget this and think that you can do things without my knowledge. That is when you get into trouble. Dharmaraj's ignorance was that he thought he can play the game of dice without my knowledge. If Dharmaraj had realized that I am always present with everyone in the form of 'Sakshi' (witness), then the game would have finished differently'

Uddhava was spellbound and got overwhelmed by Bhakti. 'What a deep philosophy. What a great truth! Even praying and doing pooja to God and calling Him for help are nothing but our feeling and belief. When we start believing that nothing moves without Him, how can we not feel his presence as Witness? How can we forget this and act? Throughout Bhagavad Gita, this is the philosophy Krishna imparted to Arjuna. He was the charioteer as well as guide for Arjuna, but he did not fight on his own.'-

Realize that Ultimate Sakshi/ Witnesser within &
without you! And Merge in that God-Consciousness!
Discover Thy Higher Self- the Pure Love full &
Blissful Supreme Consciousness! - Tat Tvam Asi!

Lord Krishna's Fish Form (Matshy Rupa)

Matsya (Fish in Sanskrit) was the first avatar of Vishnu. The great flood finds mention in the ancients' texts like the Satapatha Brahmana, wherein the Matsya Avatar takes place to save the pious and the first man, Manu. Lord Matsya is generally represented as a four-armed figure with the upper torso of a man and the lower of a fish.

This is the account of the Lord Krishna's previous incarnation as a fish. The Vedas are thought to have been taken from Lord Brahma by the demon Hayagriva. According to legend, during the Satya Yuga, humanity had degenerated into an irreligious and disorderly race. At this point, the Gods made the decision to flood the world to prepare it for reconstruction.

Lord Vishnu had provided Lord Brahma, the creator, with instructions on how to redesign the earth. The four guiding principles books were the Vedas. The creator, Lord Brahma, chose to take a break before beginning this important duty because he was quite worn out from the act of creation.

The Vedas were being held by Brahma when a demon with a horse's head named Hayagriva emerged from his nose. A King by the name of Satyavrata Maharaj lived at about the same time. A small fish begged King Satyavrata, the prehistoric Dravida king and a follower of Vishnu who subsequently took the name Manu, to preserve its life as he was washing his hands in a river. He placed it in a jar, which Satyavrata soon outgrew. Then, to no use, he transported it to a tank, a river, and last, the ocean. The fish then showed himself to be Vishnu and informed the man that an apocalyptic flood will wipe out all life within seven days.

The fish informed Manu that the horse who dwelt at the bottom of the ocean would open her lips and spew a lethal fire at the conclusion of the Kaliyuga. The entire cosmos, all the gods, the constellations, everything, will be consumed by this fire. The earth would thereafter be flooded by the seven clouds of doom until it was covered by a single ocean.

Therefore, the fish instructed Satyavrata to build an ark to take "all medicinal herbs, all the varieties of seeds, and accompanied by the seven saints (Saptarishis)" along with the serpent Vasuki and other animals.

As the time of the flood approached, Manu's ark was complete. As the flood swept over the land, Manu asked Vishnu why humanity had to meet such a deadly fate to which Matsya Vishnu told Manu that he was the only moral man alive and that he would be the father of the future generations of men. Matsya killed Hayagriva and returned the Vedas to Brahma. Then he tied himself to Manu's ark using Vasuki as a rope and protected them from the storm and the floods.

The Supreme Lord is situated in everyone's heart and thus Lord taught the king all about Vedic knowledge from the core of the heart. When the storms ended and the water subsided, Matsya Vishnu left Manu and the others at the Himalayas, where they could begin human civilization again.

God is in the form of a Dwarf man (Vamana Rupa)

According to the Bhagavata Purana, Lord Vishnu descended in the Vamana avatar to reinstate Indra's rule as the King of the Heavens after Mahabali, an asura, had usurped it. Prahlada, a well-known devotee of Vishnu, had a grandson by the name of Bali.

The world praised King Mahabali for his generosity, extreme penance, and harsh austerities. Vamana went to the monarch to ask for three paces of land while posing as a Brahmin and carrying a wooden cloak. Despite his guru's caution, Mahabali gave his approval. Bali Maharaj did a fire sacrifice.

Shukracharya gave him a conch shell, and Prahlada Maharaj, Bali Maharaj's grandfather, gave him an everlasting flower garland. After bowing down to Prahlada Maharaj, the Brahmanas, and his spiritual guide Shukracarya, Bali Maharaj armed himself for battle with Indra and headed to IndraPuri with his troops. When Indra learned of Bali Maharaj's skill, he proceeded to consult his own spiritual leader,

Brihaspati, who counseled the gods to abandon the celestial planets.

Shukracharya gave him a conch shell, and Prahlada Maharaj, Bali Maharaj's grandfather, gave him an everlasting flower garland. After bowing down to Prahlada Maharaj, the Brahmanas, and his spiritual guide Shukracarya, Bali Maharaj armed himself for battle with Indra and headed to IndraPuri with his troops. When Indra learned of Bali Maharaj's skill, he proceeded to consult his own spiritual leader, Brihaspati, who counseled the gods to abandon the celestial planets.

Then, Lord Vamanadeva went to Bali Maharaj's sacrifice area. All the priests rose from their seats and prayed to Him due to His transcendentally effulgent presence. Bali Maharaj consented to donate three paces of land as charity when Lord Vamanadeva asked for it. Shukracharya advised Bali Maharaj to back out of his commitment. Then Lord Vamanadeva revealed who he was and grew enormously to walk over the three worlds. He took the first step from heaven to earth. The inability to carry out his vow led

King Mahabali to take his third step by offering his head. As a reward for the king's humility, Vamana then stepped forward and bestowed immortality. Bali Maharaj was provided protection by Supreme Lord Vamana Deva, in giant form, Vamana is known as Trivikrama.

The Incarnation of Rama

According to the Shrimad Bhagavatam, Lord Maha Vishnu received prayers for the establishment of dharma on earth from all the demigods and celestial beings, including Lord Brahma and Lord Shiva. The Lord decided to come to earth after hearing the celestials' requests. He then expands himself into four pieces by his capacity of plenary expansions becoming Rama, Bharata, Lakshmana, and Shatrughna, who were all born to Dasharatha, the king of Ayodhya. When he was a child, Rama vanquished the demons that were destroying the sacrifices of the sage Vishwamitra.

It's fascinating and unusual to see Lord Vishnu in this form. Only God can demonstrate what an ideal human should do and how they should live because only God created people. God (Lord Rama) assumed human form on this planet to serve as the best possible example of how a perfect human should act and live. The goal of this incarnation was to eliminate Ravana and free the planet from his wicked deeds.

Ravana offered Brahma a lengthy period of rigorous penance (or Tapasya). As part of his penance, Ravana sacrificed his head ten times to make him happy. He was able to continue his penance since new heads kept emerging every time, he chopped off one. After his tenth decapitation, Brahma finally showed up, satisfied with his piety, and gave him a blessing. Ravana requested absolute invulnerability from and dominance over gods, heavenly spirits, other rakshasas, serpents, and wild animals in place of immortality, which Brahma refused to grant. He did not want protection from these since he was contemptuous of mortal mankind. Along with his ten severed heads and enormous strength, Brahma bestowed upon him these blessings through his understanding of heavenly weaponry and magic. As a result, Ravana is often referred to as "Dasamukha" or "Dashaanan" (Dasa = ten, mukha = face).

Ravana could only have been murdered by a human. For this reason, Rama genuinely assumes the form of a human and behaves in accordance with all human emotions. He is God manifested as a person. acting within the bounds of humanity.

He acquired Sita as his bride with ease after breaking Shiva's bow. Rama ran into Parashuraam on his way back from the wedding, but he quickly defeated the formidable warrior. A few years later, in order to uphold Dasharatha's promise, Rama, Sita, and Lakshmana departed for the forest and a fourteen-year exile.

After learning about Sita's beauty through his sister Surpanakha, the king of Lanka, Ravana, went to the forest and abducted her. Then, with the assistance of Lord Hanuman, Lord Rama discovered that Sita was in Lanka.

Rama and Lakshmana marched alongside a sizable army of monkeys and bears to the shore, where the sea god urged them to construct a bridge that would allow them to travel to Lanka. They all crossed over after constructing the bridge to launch their assault on Lanka. The army of Ravana was swiftly defeated by

Rama's army using trees, mountain tops, clubs, and arrows. At last, Ravana was killed by Lord Ram.

It is believed, Lord Ram worshiped Lord Shiva in south India, and ever since that time, the lingam of Lord Shiva is called Rameshvaram. (The Lord worshipped by Rama).

Rama himself crowned Vibhishana, the good brother of Ravana who had aided Rama, king of Lanka. Now that his fourteen-year exile was over, Rama returned to Ayodhya in an aerial chariot with Sita, Lakshmana, Sugriva, Hanuman, and other companions.

Bharata, Rama's younger brother, who had led the country during those fourteen years, was ecstatic to hear of his brother's return. Bharata had been subsisting on a meager diet for all that time, dressing only in bark, and sleeping on the ground. He carried Rama's sandals along with Shatrughna as they proceeded to welcome Rama. They were accompanied by all the people, some waving banners, flagstaffs, and other royal emblems, while others were singing Vedic chants. Bharata knelt before his brother, laying Rama's sandals at his feet, his eyes streaming with sorrow. Rama was then anointed king of Ayodhya, where he reigned wisely and compassionately for many years over all his subjects.

The twin sons Lava and Kusha were born at the ashrama of the Sage Valmiki. Sita left her sons in Valmiki's care and descended to the planet where she was born. Even without his wife, Rama continued to make pious sacrifices and rule Ayodhya for many years before entering his own Supreme State.

Because of this, Lord Rama is a unique and remarkable incarnation (avatar) of the All-Powerful God. It is true that when acting as a human, Lord Rama was unaware of his divinity. He couldn't have acted like a human if he had known. He remains divine despite this. He is the ultimate Lord Vishnu himself, who gave permission to Yogamaya to disguise his divinity and give the impression that he is a mortal. In actuality, the fact that in this Lila He was unaware of his own divinity adds to its intrigue and excitement.

He was a human at birth. Like other people, he offered sacrifices to the gods. He carried out his human dharma and karma to the letter. Then, one bright day, he vanquishes a demon with ten heads that even demigods never could conquer.

All the demigods' celestials told him that he is a divine being. Still, he identifies himself as the son of his mortal father. A perfect end to a perfect human being's life.

Therefore, Lord Rama is truly a divine incarnation. God created humans, therefore only God can display and model how a perfect human should live and act. Hence, he is also called Purushottam. (The Perfect Human)

The Story of Parashuraam

According to the Shrimad Bhagavatam (SB 9.16), Lord Parashuraam formed a horrific river using the blood from the bodies of these sons, which greatly frightened the monarchs who had no regard for brahminical culture. In retaliation for his father's murder, Lord Parashuraam exterminated all the kshatriyas (administrative and warrior class), the men in positions of authority, twenty-one times because they engaged in wicked behavior.

In fact, he drained their blood into nine lakes and built them in the region known as Samanta-panchaka. One of the duties of Godhead incarnation is to murder all sinful men. Because they disobeyed the brahminical customs, Lord Parashuraam slew every kshatriya 21 times in a row. The claim that the kshatriyas murdered his father was just a defense; the truth is that the kshatriyas, the governing class, were inauspicious because of their unclean state.

This question was asked by Parikshit Maharaj to the sage Sukadeva. Sri Shuka said: There was at this time a sage named Jamadagni who had several sons, the youngest of whom was Parashuraam, who destroyed the line of Kshatriyas twenty-one times.

King Parikshit asked: What was the offence that the Kshatriyas did that would cause such terrible retribution?

Sage Shuka replied: The monarch of that region at the time was a strongman by the name of Arjuna (not to confuse with Arjun from the Mahabharata), who after worshiping Dattatreya gained a thousand arms and many other benefits. No one could stop him because he could fly anywhere in the world. When Parashuraam was gone, he once sent his troops to Jamadagni ashrama. With the aid of Kamadhenu, the celestial wish-fulfilling cow, the sage Jamadagni greeted the king and his attendants and started off by providing them with regal entertainment.

Arjuna, however, turned down the sage's invitation out of conceit and withdrew. Arjuna dispatched some soldiers to catch Kamadhenu and bring her to him when he got back to his city. After that, the men proceeded to the ashrama and abducted Kamadhenu and her calf. Arjuna was the ruler of that area at the time, and because of his worship of Dattatreya, he attained a thousand weapons and many other advantages. He could fly anywhere in the world; thus no one could stop him.

Then Arjuna arrived carrying mountains and trees to fight Parashuraam, but once more Parashuraam destroyed everything with his axe. Then he severed Arjuna's arms one by one before killing him by chopping off his head.

When Arjuna's ten thousand sons witnessed the destruction caused by Parashuraam, they all ran away. Then, after locating Kamadhenu and her calf, Parashuraam returned them to the ashrama.

Jamadagni reprimanded Parashuraam, saying, "O Rama, you have committed a sin," when he entered the ashrama and informed his father and brothers of what he had done. You murdered a king who contained all the divinities without cause. As Brahmans, we. Our superiority is a result of our patience. Our strength comes from our patience. Jamadagni then instructed his son to atone for this sin by visiting sacred locations, engaging in yoga, and focusing on the Lord during meditation.

After Parashuraam had returned from his trip a few years later, he found out, Arjuna's sons came to the ashrama to get revenge on their father one day while he was once more outside with his brothers. They hacked off Jamadagni's head and brought it away after observing him reclining in meditation. Parashuraam hurried back to the ashrama after hearing his mother's wailing even from a considerable distance away.

When he saw his father's body, he was horrified and furious. He gave the body to his brothers and then left with his axe to wipe off all Kshatriyas from the planet. He killed practically all the Kshatriyas after twenty-one expeditions, at which point he stopped. Then, after locating his father's head, he set it on the trunk and started a significant sacrifice. He gave over all the lands he had acquired to the sacrifice makers and their helpers. After the sacrifice, Jamadagni came back to life and eventually evolved into one of the seven sages known as saptarishis.

As Parashuraam, the Lord's sixteenth manifestation,

He destroyed the Kshatriyas (the ruling class) twenty-one times out of wrath for their uprising against the Brahmanas (the intelligent class). The intelligent class of men, who give guidance to the rulers in terms of the accepted sastras, or the books of revealed knowledge, are expected to direct the Kshatriyas, or the administrative class of men, in ruling the world. The rulers continue to run the country in that direction. Every time the Kshatriyas, or the administrative class, disobey the knowledgeable and intellectual brahmanas' directives, the administrators are forcibly removed from their positions, and plans are created for improved administration.

Vidura Meets Uddhava & Maitreya.

The great sage Sukadeva was delighted to see King Parikshit's eagerness. Though the king had only seven days to live, he showed no fear of death. Sukadeva then began to tell the story of the Kauravas and Pandavas. Dhritarashtra, the blind king, wanting to please his wicked sons, allowed them to torture and persecute the Pandavas, his nephews. He even allowed his sons to burn the Pandavas' house down while they were in it. And he also allowed them to humiliate their noble wife Draupadi before the royal court. Finally, Dhritarashtra's eldest son Duryodhana, drove the Pandavas into exile in the forest, cheating them out of all their worldly possessions in a crooked game of dice.

Dhritarashtra had a brother named Vidura, who was wise and righteous. Vidura wanted to divert his brother from his evil ways and bring him to the right path, so he advised Dhritarashtra to disown his evil son Duryodhana. This made Shakuni and other friends of Duryodhana extremely angry. Duryodhana heaped abuse upon Vidura and drove him from the court. Vidura no longer wanted to live in the city of Hastinapur, so he left the palace, dressed in humble clothes, and set out on a long pilgrimage.

After many years, even after Kurukshetra war, he happened to meet Sri Krishna's beloved friend, Uddhava. When Vidura asked him about Sri Krishna, Uddhava, who had been devoted to the Lord since childhood, began to weep. He said, 'Sri Krishna has ended his sport here on earth, and has left for his own abode.' He then began to relate many stories of Krishna's life—how he was born, how he killed the demon Kamsa, how he played with the Gopis in Vrindavan, and so on. Then, after relating how Krishna gave his final teachings to him before leaving the world,

Uddhava said: 'The pain of separation from him is unbearable. Now I am going, at the Lord's command, to Badrikashrama to spend my days in meditation on him.' Seeing Vidura's grief at getting the news of Krishna's passing away, Uddhava said: 'Sri Krishna has asked the rishi Maitreya to instruct you. Please go to him.'

Seeing Vidura, a great devotee of the Lord, Maitreya felt great joy. Maitreya told him about how God incarnates himself on earth as an avatar and about the creation of the universe. He explained that before creation, there is just absolute Consciousness existing, nothing else. This Consciousness is identical to God. Through the power of God's Maya, the universe manifests, making that one absolute Consciousness appear as many. Vidura, the best amongst the Kuru dynasty, who was perfect in devotional service to the Lord, thus reached the source of the celestial Ganges River [Haridwar], where Maitreya, the great, fathomless learned sage of the world, was seated. Vidura, who was perfect in gentleness and satisfied in transcendence, inquired from him. Vidura asks questions to the great sage as follows.

Everyone in this world engages in fruitive activities to attain happiness, but one finds neither satiation nor the mitigation of distress. On the contrary, one is only aggravated by such activities. Please, therefore, give us directions on how one should live for real happiness.

Please give me instruction on the transcendental devotional service of the Lord, so that the god within us will be pleased and shed the knowledge of the Absolute Truth in terms of the ancient Vedic principles delivered only to those who are purified by the process of devotional service.

Kindly narrate how the Supreme Personality of Godhead, who is the independent, desireless Lord of the three worlds and the controller of all energies, accepts incarnations and creates the cosmic manifestation with perfectly arranged regulative principles for its maintenance.

You may narrate also about the auspicious characteristics of the Lord in His different incarnations for the welfare of the twice-born, the cows and the demigods. Our minds are never satisfied completely, although we continuously hear of His transcendental activities.

Please also describe how Narayana, the creator of the universe and the self-sufficient Lord, has differently

created the natures, activities, forms, features, and
names of the different living creatures.

Kindly describe the essence of all topics-the topics of
the Lord. Kindly chant all those superhuman
transcendental activities of the Supreme Controller,
the Personality of Godhead, who accepted
incarnations fully equipped with all potency for the
full manifestation and maintenance of the cosmic
creation.

Sri Maitreya said: O Vidura, all glory unto you. You
have inquired from me of the greatest of all goodness,
and thus you have shown your love for the supreme
Lord.

Seeing Vidura, a great devotee of the Lord, Maitreya
felt great joy. Maitreya told him about how God
incarnates himself on earth as an avatar with his
plenary expansions and about the creation of the
universe. He explained that before creation, there is
just absolute Consciousness existing, nothing else.
This Consciousness is identical to God. Through the
power of God's Maya, the universe manifests, making

that one absolute Consciousness appear as many.

There are three kinds of devotees—the neophyte devotee, the intermediate devotee and the advanced devotee.

As per SB 3.24.46, That everyone is existing on the Supreme Personality of Godhead does not mean that everyone is also Godhead. This is also explained in Bhagavad-gītā: everything is resting on Him, the Supreme Lord, but that does not mean that the Supreme Lord is also everywhere. This mysterious position has to be understood by highly advanced devotees.

There are three kinds of devotees—the neophyte devotee, the intermediate devotee, and the advanced devotee. The neophyte devotee does not understand the techniques of devotional science, but simply offers devotional service to the Deity in the temple; the intermediate devotee understands who God is, who is a devotee, who is a non-devotee and who is innocent, and he deals with such persons differently. But a person who sees that the Lord is sitting as

Paramātmā in everyone's heart and that everything is depending or existing on the transcendental energy of the Supreme Lord is in the highest devotional position.

Akrura's Meeting with Krishna and Balarama

Akrura, a minister of Kansa was also a blood relative of Krishna. He was a great devotee of Lord Krishna. Kansa had invited Krishna and Balaram for the 'worship of Bow' ceremony and had sent Akrura to escort them. Akrura was an ardent devotee of Krishna, his heart was so focused on Krishna that throughout the journey to Vrindavan, he thought only of Krishna.

After the killing of Aristasura by the Lord Krishna, the sage Narada came to King Kamsa and instigated by informing and reminding him about Krishna and Balaram, who are living in Vraj. They supposed to be the annihilator of Kamsa.

Kamsa announced to hold a "Bow-yajna" and planned to invite Krishna and Balarama to the yajna. Simultaneously he planned to kill Krishna & Balarama by his elephants, wrestlers, and other demons through a yajna of celebration a wrestling match. Meanwhile, Kamsa also sent two more demons, one after the

other, to try to kill Balarama and Krishna. But both—
Keshi, the horse demon, and Vyoma—were quickly
killed by Krishna.

Kamsa summons Akrura was a well-respected
member of the royal Yadu family. Directs him to
escort Krishna and Balarama. The next day Akrura
went in a beautiful chariot to Vraja to bring Krishna
and Balarama to Mathura. Being a great devotee of
the Lord, his happiness was knowing no bounds.
When he reached the Vrindavan, he saw Krishna's
footsteps on the sand. He was so overcome with
devotion he rolled himself on the great one's foot
marks. Such was his love for the greatness of Krishna.
Indeed, he was a spiritually ascended one to recognize
the higher state of Lord Krishna.

He was very joyous to accompany both Krishna and
Balarama on their way to Mathura. On the way
Akrura stopped the chariot and cautioned them to be
careful as he went to the Yamuna River for
worshipping. When he dipped his head in the water,
he saw forms of Krishna and Balarama inside the
water. It was bewildering; he looked back to the

chariot and saw both sitting there. Imagining that he was only hallucinating he dipped back into the water. This time he saw Lord Krishna in his divine form, Akrura felt, the Lord blessed him to have a vision of his grand form.

Akrura was so eager to see the two boys that his mind reflected repeatedly, with great longing, on how he would greet them and how they would greet him when they met. When he arrived, his wish came true. Nanda cordially welcomed him, and Balarama and Krishna washed his feet and gave other offerings. He was treated to a sumptuous feast. Akrura then said: 'I have come to invite you to the bow-yajna, with all the related festivities. But I must reveal to you the hidden motive behind this apparently cordial invitation. Kamsa is planning to kill Krishna and Balarama using this invitation as a ruse. 'When Krishna and Balarama heard this, they laughed and replied: 'Very well, we accept this invitation, and shall go to Mathura.' Nanda and other Gopas also decided to go. When the Gopis heard the heart-rending news that Krishna would go away to Mathura, they were stricken with grief. But

Krishna and Balarama were destined to leave for Mathura.

The next day the chariot was made ready. Nanda and other boys and men also mounted their carts. Despite all attempts by the Gopis to stop the chariot containing Balarama and Krishna, it left for Mathura, carrying the two brothers, along with Akrura.

On the way, Akrura halted the chariot by the Yamuna. They all got down, saw the beautiful riverbank, touched Yamuna's waters, and quenched their thirst. Akrura then brought Krishna and Balarama back to the chariot, and he went for a holy bath in the river. When Akrura went under the water, he was astonished to see Krishna and Balarama there. 'Aren't they in the chariot?' he thought. Then he came up for air and verified before submerged again in the water. This time he saw Supreme Person Maha Vishnu, seated on the divine serpent Ananta Naga. radiating peace, bliss, and all auspicious qualities. Akrura was struck dumb and subdued and tears rolled down his cheeks. He started reciting the hymns to praise the lord. He finished his bath and came back to the chariot. Acting as if he knew nothing, Krishna asked: 'Well, what happened to you? You look as though you have seen something wonderful!' Akrura replied, 'Whatever wonderful things there are in this world, they all exist in you alone!' Akrura then got in the chariot, and they continued to Mathura.

How merciful is the supreme lord, He personally comes to the devotee and showers his blessings. One who experiences eternal sight, will forget all material desires and everything and raise to the next level in the love of Krishna. No one can understand the Maya of Krishna and Balarama except themselves.

The Birth of Sri Krishna

Sukadeva read the Bhagavatam stories to King Parikshit as he prepared for his impending demise. "I am drinking the nectar of the holy words coming from your lotus lips," the king declared. To me, everything you have said about Sri Hari is nectar. I am on a fast. I do not even have any water. Despite that, I am not in any pain. Please tell me in detail about the history of Sri Krishna's birth and his earlier years.

"I am very happy to see your deep interest in the story of Sri Krishna," Sukadeva retorted. Even one who shares this tale is fortunate. Questions about the Lord purify these three: the one who asks the question, the one who answers it, and the one who hears the response, just as holy water from the Ganga purifies everyone. The narrator, the hearer, and the questioner are all made pure by Sri Krishna's words. "I am very happy to see your deep interest in the story of Sri Krishna," Sukadeva retorted. Even one who shares this tale is fortunate. Questions about the Lord purify these three, including the one who asks the question, and the one who receives the answer, just as the holy water of the Ganga purifies everyone.

He tells the tale as follows: "One day, the mother earth assumed the form of a cow and, weeping bitterly, told Brahma of her woes: "I am terribly oppressed by hundreds of tyrannical kings and their retinues of demon soldiers. I cannot take it any longer. Please act. Lord Brahma contemplated Maha Vishnu after hearing the earth's wailing plea. Finally, he felt the Lord's voice speaking to him from within, saying, "I am already aware of the misery of the earth. Soon, I will be born in Vasudeva's home. The demigods and their wives will be born on earth in the interim, carrying a portion of their essence. The first to arrive will be Ananta Deva with his thousand heads. Even my power of Maya will also descend to fulfill a certain purpose.'

In Mathura, Vasudeva was born into the Yadu royal family. He eventually wed Devaki, a cousin of King Kamsa. Following the wedding, Kamsa himself drove Devaki and Vasudeva's chariot as it transported them back to Vasudeva's house. Kamsa abruptly heard a voice saying, "O Kamsa, you fool! You are riding in this chariot with Devaki. But this Devaki's eighth child will murder you! Evil Kamsa quickly grabbed Devaki by her hair and pulled out his sword, ready to take her life after hearing this celestial prophecy. Vasudeva intervened to save the life of his young bride, remarking, "How can you think of killing your sister, and that too at the time of her marriage celebration? It is not Devaki who is going to kill you. If the words uttered by that heavenly voice are true, then your killer will be her eighth child. Why then commit the sin of killing an innocent woman? I give you my word that I will hand over to you all the children born to Devaki, and you do whatever you please with them.'

These words calmed Kamsa, who then released Devaki. But Kamsa's fear of dying persisted. It is said that you should not let your adversaries live. Considering this, Kamsa imprisoned Devaki and Vasudeva. Kamsa killed each child as it was being born to them. In the meantime, the Mathura people were being terrorized by Kamsa, who had turned into a brutal despot. To succeed to the throne, he even put his own father in prison.

The due date for Balarama, Devaki's seventh child, was rapidly approaching. "O Devi, go to Devaki, take the unborn child from her womb, and place it in the womb of Rohini, who is staying in Vraja, in Nanda's camp," Sri Bhagavan instructed Yogamaya. Then, I will be born as Devaki's son and you will be born as Yashoda's daughter. Balarama was soon born to Rohini in Vraja after Yogamaya carried out the Lord's instructions.

The eighth child of Devaki will be born at this time. It was dark. In Kamsa's prison, Devaki and Vasudeva were present. Bhagavan Sri Krishna was born at a moment that was extraordinarily auspicious. However, what did the worried parents see? Standing in front of them, Sri Vishnu himself was holding a conch, mace, chakra, and lotus in each of his four hands while illuminating the dark prison with his radiant presence. Overwhelmed, the parents fell to their knees while singing praising hymns. I was twice born to you, Sri Bhagavan remarked with pleasure.

You will ascend to higher and higher stages of divine love and reach my state if you consider me to be the supreme Brahman and your son. Vishnu then took the supreme lord has descended to earth as a human on earth, but we need to understand the human form has certain limitations, rules, and regulations, just like when we go to a different city or country on earth, we must obey their rules and regulations. Therefore, the Supreme lord must obey these rules and regulations within his human form.

In fear of Kamsa, who would kill him, Vasudeva decided to travel to Vraja while holding the infant in his arms. It was pitch black. There was torrential rain. The weather was not ideal for this mother and newborn to flee to Vraj. He observes this here! The prison guards fell asleep thanks to Yogamaya's power, and the locked gates automatically opened. The father and child were shielded from the rain by Ananta, the thousand-headed serpent, who was standing behind Vasudeva.

Vasudeva arrived at the Yamuna River, but due to the intense rain, it has strong currents. Vasudeva was able to cross the Yamuna when its waters abruptly split. He then traveled to Vraja, Nanda's cowherd village, and went inside Nanda and Yashoda's residence. Yogamaya was born that same night as the daughter of Nanda and Yashoda, but because Yogamaya had put Yashoda to sleep, the mother was unaware of the gender of the child when she gave birth to it. The girl was discovered by her sleeping mother Vasudeva. He gently laid the divine baby by Yashoda's side, took the girl baby in his arms, and returned to the prison, where the gates locked automatically behind him. There he placed the baby girl in Devaki's arms. Such was the Maya of Yogamaya that no one found out about Vasudeva's mission.

When the baby girl started crying, the prison guards were alerted. They told Devaki to tell Kamsa about the baby. Immediately. The girl was taken from Devaki by the ruthless Kamsa who arrived. She flew out of his hand and rose into the air just as he was about to dash the infant to death on a stone slab. She appeared as an eight-armed goddess and questioned the point of her own death. Your assailant is not here.

Stop murdering innocent kids. The goddess then vanished.

Yogamaya, who is regarded as the universe's material cause, serves as a liaison between Shri Krishna and his followers. One of Shri Krishna's supra powers, Yogamaya, enables him to plan and organize events beyond what is possible for humans. He gains the ability to do things that are unexpected and unimaginable thanks to this power. Because of this, he is referred to as Yogeshwar, the supreme authority in yoga. We can achieve the goal of life—union with Shri Krishna—through Yogamaya's grace. She leads us toward our goal as we submit to her, and she aids us in overcoming every challenge we face along the way. In essence, Yogamaya is a symbol of the divine feminine energy that permeates the entire cosmos and guides.

Guru-Dakshina of Krishna and Balarama

The primary responsibility of a teacher in the modern era is to teach students the fundamentals of subjects like Mathematics, Science, English, and others. A teacher or guru, on the other hand, was a spiritually advanced leader in ancient India. Along with imparting knowledge on a variety of topics, he also showed his pupils how to lead a disciplined life based on moral principles. A guru served as his students' spiritual mentor and life coach. Gurudakshina is an extremely old idea that is only found in Indian culture and tradition.

A famous teacher by the name of Sandipani lived in Avantipur and was a sage. Krishna and Balarama went to study under him after the appropriate rites. Krishna and Balarama served the sage Sandipani just like the other students did, and despite their great deeds—killing Putana, taming Kaliya, and killing Kamsa—they were modest in their demeanor and polite to their teacher. They were instructed in the

Vedas and Upanishads by Sandipani, who was pleased with them. After that, they studied dharma, ethics, logic, politics, the art of running a kingdom, war rules, and other related topics. They were experts at everything. They were able to focus so well that they mastered all 64 subjects in just 64 days. Their training was over at that point.

They then asked their guru to accept a gift, or guru-dakshina, as a form of homage. The wise man talked to his wife. "What should I demand of them?" God has come to me for instruction. Being their teacher is an honor for me. Well, at Prabhasa, our lone son perished in the sea. Let us ask Krishna and Balarama to revive our son if they are really God.

The two brothers hurried to Prabhasa, which is by the sea, to fulfill the sage's wish. The sea god arrived and bowed at Krishna and Balarama's feet after learning that the Lord himself had appeared to him as them. "O Sea, you have swallowed the son of my guru with your tremendous waves," declared Krishna. Bring him back now.

The Sea God retorted, "That boy was not swallowed by me. It was Panchajanya, an asura who takes the shape of a conch and resides in my water. There was no boy in the demon's stomach when Krishna dove into the sea to find and kill the monster. The conch, which had been a component of the asura's body, was brought back by him. Then he followed Balarama to Yama, Death's residence. He blew the Panchajanya conch there loudly. "O Lord, both of you are incarnations of Vishnu himself, and you have taken human form in your divine play, your Lila," Yama hurriedly exclaimed. Please let me know how I can help you.

The son of my guru has passed away, because of his karma, you have brought him here,' Krishna retorted. This was correct. You made the right decision. But now I must tell you to give him back. The king of Death agreed right away.

Krishna and Balarama then brought their guru's son back to his home. The guru and his wife were immensely happy and wholeheartedly blessed the two brothers. Krishna and Balarama, endowed with the blessings of their guru, returned to Mathura and its citizens, who were overjoyed to have them back.

Gopis' Complain to Uddhava.

After returning from his guru's house, Krishna spent some time in Mathura. Meanwhile, in Vrindavan, the Gopis were despondent. Mother Yashoda and Nanda were also anxious to see their darling sons, Krishna, and Balarama, so Krishna wanted to send Uddhava as a messenger to Vrindavan.

Krishna's beloved cousin (and the son of his father's brother) was Uddhava. Aside from the other servants, he was serving Shri Krishna as well. When Uddhava learned of Shri Krishna's sadness, he immediately began to reflect. He reasoned that if Shri Krishna had access to all comforts—servants, delectable food, prosperity, and wealth—then what was it that made him feel so sad? Uddhava was a man of spiritual wisdom but his heart was without bhakti. Shri Krishna decided to send Uddhava to Gokul to learn bhakti from Gopis so that his spiritual wisdom would fructify. Simultaneously, Gopis would also gain spiritual wisdom and it will reduce the pain of separation. Uddhava was instructed by Shri Krishna to travel to Vraj and teach the locals about Vedanta while pleading with them to forget about him. He would forget them as soon as they did. Krishna told Uddhava, "You should go to Vrindavan and teach the Gopis to forget him." Because Vraj needs a wise man, Uddhava reasoned, he should be sent there. "He is ready to go, but how would the uneducated people of Vraj understand Vedanta," Uddhava said. Therefore, going there would be pointless. "Gopis are beyond education but have learned love; they have sacrificed their husbands, relatives, etc.," said Shri Krishna. The Gopies need the wisdom, Uddhava. So, he must leave. Uddhava didn't want to go, but he did so to fulfill Shri Krishna's wish.

After arriving at night in Vrindavan, Nanda warmly welcomed Uddhava. 'Does Krishna still remember us?' Nanda asked. 'And when does he plan to come back and see us? His memory haunts us. We think about him so much that we neglect our own work.' Nanda then continued: 'Balarama and Krishna are two divine beings who have come to earth. Just think: Krishna killed Kamsa and the wrestler Chanara effortlessly as if they had been a dog and a cat. He broke Kamsa's huge bow into pieces like an elephant snapping off a sugar cane. He saved us from the flood unleashed by Indra, holding Mount Govardhan in his left hand for a week.'

Nanda and Uddhava went on and on talking about Krishna until the anguish of Nanda's grief became too much for him to bear. Yashoda also, who was listening to them speak, could not control her tears. Seeing their love for Krishna, Uddhava said: 'O great ones! You have attained the highest form of devotion to that Being, the Supreme Narayana, who is the soul of all. What another end is there left for you to achieve? Surely Krishna will come soon to see you. Do not grieve.'

Uddhava heard the Krishna bhajan of Gopis while taking a bath in Yamuna. He believed that Vraj people are fortunate to sing Krishna's bhajan in the morning and that Gopis sing so beautifully. Slowly, Uddhava's pride in his knowledge faded. Later, Gopis was chatting about Shri Krishna among themselves. When she tries to forget Kanhaiya, he returns to her mind more strongly; yesterday, she saw him playing the flute on the tree and went slightly insane; as a result, she tied her child instead of a bucket and dropped him in the well; Kanhaiya pulled him out of the well. People may say whatever they want, but the woman is certain that Kanhaiya is the only one here. Yesterday, when she was approaching a well in the dark and frightened, Kanhaiya chatted with her and approached her.

The next morning the women of Vrindavan went to see Uddhava as he was returning from his morning ablutions. The Gopis said to him: 'We understand that you attend on Krishna. We are sure he has sent you to find out how his parents are keeping him. He must have forgotten all about us. But then, why wouldn't he? As soon as their needs are met, subjects leave the king behind, disciples leave the guru behind, and the priest leaves the worshipper behind. The birds leave the tree when the fruit is gone. Guests leave a banquet when the feast is over. So, it is not surprising that Krishna would leave us.' Though speaking in such strains, the Gopis could not hold back their tears of love and anguish.

Gopis and Nand-Yashoda, according to Uddhava see Krishna in everything and everywhere. They perceive God as omnipresent, and he spent a great deal of time thinking about God. He was caught up in Vedantic doctrines but was unable to encounter the Almighty. His entire sense of brilliance evaporated.

Uddhava was brought before Radhika by Gopis. Radhika was in a terrible state. "Shri Krishna is here only and everywhere," she added again. "He has brought a message of Krishna," Uddhava reaffirmed. My Krishna is everywhere, in my heart, and throughout my entire being, Radhika declared. Uddhava asked Radhika to give him Premlakshna Bhakti so that his mind wouldn't become dull from arrogance. Radhika gave in.

To comfort them, Uddhava said: 'You have devoted yourselves solely to Krishna, who is the Lord himself. I bow to all of you. You see, it is not easy to acquire devotion to the Lord. The sages undertake a lot of penance, meditation, and Japa, but they still do not get this kind of devotion. You all are so fortunate that you have acquired such deep devotion to Krishna.

Moreover, you have surrendered your minds completely to him. It is good fortune earned over many lifetimes to be able to leave everything behind and worship the greatest of all beings, Sri Krishna. I have brought a message from your beloved one.

Please listen. Here is what the Lord said to tell you: "'You can never be separated from Me, since I permeate the entire universe, including your minds and bodies. I dwell within all as the Self. I create, sustain, and dissolve everything within myself and out of myself by my Maya power. I know I am everything to you. I am your all in all. And yet, I am staying so far away from you. This has a reason. When you do not get to see me with your eyes, you will devote your entire mind to me. You will forever meditate on me. Through meditation, you all will be united with me.'"

The Gopis, however, could not be consoled. Though knowing in their minds that what Krishna had said was true, yet his words could not relieve the anguish of their hearts. To comfort the Gopis, Uddhava lived in Vrindavan for a few months. The Gopis' devotion opened his eyes and revealed to him what **ahetuki** bhakti really is— that is, perfectly selfless and unfathomable devotion.

He thought: 'We are the companions of Sri Krishna, and we try to attain such love for him, but we fail. But look at these forest-dwelling women, who love Krishna. Krishna fulfilled for them the highest purpose of life through his divine dance—his Rasa Lila. I shall consider myself extremely fortunate if I am born even as a blade of grass in blessed Vrindavan where I shall be covered with the dust of the feet of these women. I repeatedly bow at their feet.'

Uddhava was taken aback. He was astonished to see Shri Krishna standing among the Gopis with his eyes fixed on everything. Uddhava had come to teach the Gopi's wisdom. He later joined the Gopis' order as a disciple. He began to identify with the Gopi. In addition to receiving spiritual wisdom from Uddhava, the Gopis also underwent a divine transformation of their Bhakti. Uddhava visited Vraj for a short time and stayed there for six months.

One can attain Lord Krishna through Bhakti. He cannot be attained by any other means. In this regard, Lord Krishna Himself states in Uddhava Gita, (11.14.20), as follows.

"My dear Uddhava, the unalloyed devotional service (Bhakti) rendered to Me by My devotees brings Me under their control. I cannot be thus attained by those engaged in practicing Yoga, studying Sankhya, performing pious work, Vedic study, austerity, or renunciation." And among all the limbs of Bhakti, the most important limb is chanting my holy names such as the Hare Krishna Maha-mantra. This is the surest and the most efficient means to attain Krishna, especially in this age of Kali-yuga.

Narada's Visit to Dwarka

In a previous life, Narada Muni was a maidservant's son. He then started working for brahmanas, earning their approval in the process. He received a spiritual body at the end of that life because of his devotional service. Then, he was born as the Lord Brahma's son. A vina was personally given to Narada Muni by the Supreme Lord. Lord Brahma gave Shrimad Bhagavatam knowledge to Narada Muni. The transcendental preacher Narada Muni travels the globe while extolling the virtues of the Supreme Lord Hari.

The sage Narada was very interested to see how Krishna spent his time because he knew that Krishna lived in Dwarka with his many wives. In Dwarka, the great architect Vishwakarma created a lovely garden with sixteen thousand homes. As soon as Narada stepped inside one of them, he saw Rukmini Devi fanning Krishna with a chamara. When Krishna saw Narada, he stood up from his seat, washed Narada's feet, and then sprinkled the water from those feet on Narada's head. Then he asked if Narada needed anything and inquired as to his wellbeing. "I am indeed lucky that I have been able to see you," Narada said with extreme politeness. All who turn to you, O Savior of the World, will find refuge in you. You can only be the subject of deva meditation. Humans can only be saved by your lotus feet from being completely submerged in misery. I am extremely fortunate to have seen those feet. Please bless me so that I will always remember them.

Narada went inside a different home. Uddhava and Krishna were playing dice there, along with another wife. As soon as Krishna spotted Narada in this location as well, he got up, washed the sage's feet, and asked if Narada needed anything. This aback took Narada. He was perplexed and wondered, "Are they the same person? The person I spoke to a short while ago and this one is undoubtedly the same person, but he acts differently.

Narada moved to the next house because he was unable to speak. He discovered Krishna holding a young child there. He observed Krishna getting ready for his bath in the home next door. As he made his way from house to house, he discovered Krishna studying the Vedas in one, performing sacrifices in another, and planning various social events for his daughter and son-in-law in a third. Again, he was performing an elaborate yajna somewhere else while worshiping the devas, who are merely aspects of himself.

Yet in other places he was busy with household activities like ordinary people, such as digging a well, consecrating a temple, or other such activities. In some places he was following a normal practice of a king and arranging to set out for hunting. Again, somewhere else he was meeting with his ministers to plan a strategic move.

Out of his own Divine play, Krishna assumed the form of a person and arrived on our planet. He was a devoted husband, a responsible father, a skilled manager, and a brave soldier all at once. The sage Narada was astounded by all the manifestations of Krishna's power. Oh Yogeshwar, I am so fortunate to see you in so many forms, he said as he bowed to the Lord. Please grant me permission to return and tell people about your multifaceted Lila.

In himself, the Lord creates and destroys. He has full expansions here. Only God can exist in all places at once and within the same frame of reference. We ignorantly contrast him with an average person. Everything that is impossible for us to imagine, consider, or think of is possible with God. We as humans maintain relationships with people in our society on a smaller scale, including those of son, daughter, mother sister, father, brother, husband, wife, and friend etc. Same person, but in various relationships, with various responsibilities and roles. Like this, God's supreme power allows him to exist in various realities, circumstances, and roles. Thanks to his plenary expansions. **Hare Krishna.**

Yashoda sees the Universe in Krishna

The young Krishna seemed to encounter miracles everywhere he went. The Vraja village residents were astounded and baffled. Mother Yashoda would occasionally worry about this, but as soon as she thought of Krishna again, she forgot about it.

She used to get complaints from her neighbors who said, "Your Gopala is always up to some mischief." For the calf to consume its mother's milk, he releases it. He shares stolen milk, curds, and butter with his friends. Even the monkeys receive them from him. Then he starts pulling our saris and braids. When we complain, he makes fun of us. Yashoda only grinned. What was left to say? She was completely aware of what they were discussing. Krishna is eating mud, said Balarama and the other cowherd boys as they ran to Yashoda one day. Krishna responded, "No, mother, I did not eat mud," when questioned about this. They are griping about me for nothing. You can determine for yourself who is right. I am opening my mouth right now.

Yashoda saw the entire universe when Krishna opened his mouth, including the sky, clouds, moon, sun, and stars; the earth, trees, rivers, and mountains; animals, people, women, and children; and even the region of Vraja and Yashoda herself. When Yashoda saw all of this in her child's mouth, she was terrified and passed out.

Each of the Lord Krishna's deeds has a purpose. Krishna was a toddler when he ate sand or mud, showing that he can obtain anything despite sin. He opened his mouth, which indicated that everything he has is dependent upon him because he is the paramatma. However, because he did not want this to affect the future in any way, he rendered his mother unconscious. However, it has also been said that anyone who is not prepared to understand the high superior knowledge... Will become unconscious

The fact that the seemingly limited can contain the unlimited is one meaning of the exchange. Only with the Supreme Lord is this accurate. At that time,

Krishna's transcendental body was small compared to the adults. Children can't eat as much because their stomachs haven't fully developed. How could that tiny form contains the entire cosmos?

Bhagavan is not constrained by the body, which is the reason. He is not subject to the dualism of spirit and matter. He embodies transcendence at its purest. The time constraint had an impact on the vision Yashoda received. One can move in and out of the Supreme Lord's stomach indefinitely. One of the foremost experts on the Ramayana, Kakabhushundi, had a comparable experience. He was ingested by the same Krishna as a young boy named Rama, the prince of Ayodhya, when he took the form of a crow.

It was reasonable for Yashoda to be worried. The emotion revealed her unadulterated love. The mother did not believe her son was invincible even though he had overcome many challenges in the past. She had no intention of stealing from Him. She was only looking to give.

Krishna has no problem eating dirt. He is open to receiving any kind of offering from His follower.

It was not necessary to have the vision of the universal form. Yashoda had already attained liberation. She didn't need persuading about the importance of her son because she was completely devoted to Him regardless of what anyone else thought or said. Nothing Krishna could possibly show her would alter their connection.

Mother Yashoda picked up the infant and began nursing Krishna by setting everything else aside. She heard the kitchen's milk suddenly boil over. She quickly lowered Gopala to the ground and dashed to the kitchen. Gopala, however, continued to nurse and grew irate. With a stone, he cracked the earthen pot containing the curds, sending the curds flying everywhere. Yashoda was shocked to see the child's destruction when she returned from the kitchen, so she went after the misbehaving child while holding a churning rod. The Lord, however, is in Bala Leela. He whom the yogis cannot reach through their worship and meditation was now being pursued by his mother. seeing his mother at last. Yashoda began using a piece of rope to bind Krishna to the husking mortar while keeping a frown on her face. She got another piece of rope and tied it to the first when she realized it was a little short, but the boy could not be tied up with it because it was still too short. Gopala's body appeared to get bigger the more rope she brought! Finally, Gopala felt sorry for her and allowed her to tie him up, demonstrating how even someone in charge of the entire universe could be restrained by the devotion of his followers.

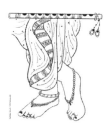

Nalakubara and Manigriva are Liberated

Sons of Kuber and followers of Shiva, Nalakubara and Manigriva. They had no regard for the rest of the world because of their conceit. They were once intoxicated and having fun with some celestial women in the river Mandakini near Mount Kailash. Soon after, Narada arrived. The women quickly changed into their clothes after seeing Narada because they felt bad about their rowdy behavior. Nalakubara and Manigriva, however, remained submerged and exposed. Oh, how inebriated and arrogant they are, Narada thought. I am going to punish these two. Allow them to become inflexible. Let them develop into two trees.

So Nalakubara and Manigriva became twin arjuna trees, and were freed from the curse by the sacred association with Krishna.

Krishna was a mortar, chained to it. Yashoda was able to move forward with her housework after the mischievous boy was moved out of her way. Young

Krishna was suddenly drawn to two arjuna trees in front of the house. He was aware that they were two of Kuber's sons who had been cursed to turn into trees. Krishna began to crawl in their direction while dragging the mortar in his wake. He was able to squeeze through the gap between the two trees, but the mortar became stuck there. He continued to pull on the mortar, though. He could not be stopped! Both trees fell to the ground with a cracking sound. Two luminous beings then emerged from the trees and approached the young Krishna.

They bowed before him and cried out, "O Lord of the Universe! We serve your servants and serve as Shiva's attendants. We are fortunate to see you today thanks to the blessing of the good association can elevate us to higher levels of consciousness, while wrong association can lead us astray. We must be vigilant in choosing our company and ensuring that it aligns with our spiritual goals. The people we surround ourselves with should inspire us to grow and evolve, rather than drag us down with negativity and distractions. By being mindful of our associations, we can cultivate a positive environment that nurtures our spiritual development. Let us strive to surround ourselves with like-minded individuals who uplift and support us on our journey toward enlightenment. O Lord, grant us your blessings: "May our lips perpetually praise your name and glory; may our ears ever hear the stories of your deeds; may our hands ever work in your service; may our minds ever be occupied with thoughts of you; may our heads ever bow before you; and may our eyes ever be occupied with gazing upon your devotees."

Lord Brahma's Doubts are Removed

After killing Aghasura, Krishna, Balarama, and their cowherd friends went to eat their food on the banks of the Yamuna River. They found a beautiful spot on the sandy bank with grass nearby for the cows. It was getting late and they were very hungry, so after tying up the cows, they all sat down to eat.

On that day, the cowherd boys feasted lavishly on Yamuna's bank while Krishna sat in the center. From above, Brahma and other devas were observing this action. Brahma was not convinced. Is this young man really Sri Vishnu, who has come to Earth to relieve it of its heavy burden? he questioned.

I will put him to the test. The calves were then lured by Brahma to a distant wood. The cowherd boys became concerned as soon as they realized the calves were missing. But Krishna assured them, "Do not be alarmed. I will see how they are. Do not interrupt your feast. Brahma kidnapped the cowherd boys and kept them hidden in a cave while Krishna was looking for the calves. Krishna eventually gave up looking for the calves and went back to the Yamuna's bank. However, Krishna wondered, "But where are Sudama, Sridama, and all the other Gopas?" He looked all over the forest but was unsuccessful in finding them. With his immense power, the supreme lord concluded that this was undoubtedly the work of the creator Brahma. Krishna changed into all the cowherd boys and the calves as a result. He adopted the characteristics of every boy and calf, including their attire, the instruments they were carrying, and names, forms, and ages.

Krishna thus demonstrated the adage "All this is Vishnu." As a result, all the "Krishna cowherd boys" and "Krishna's calves" went back to the village, where they were reunited with their respective mothers and mother cows. What joy the mothers experienced! Because Krishna, the source of all happiness, took on their roles of sons and calves. Even more than they had loved their own sons, the mothers adored their Krishna-sons! No one in Vraja suspected anything during the entire year that the Krishna-cowherd boys and Krishna-calves lived there.

Just one moment of Brahma is equivalent to one year on earth. After a moment, Brahma looked up, startled. The cowherd boys and calves are still dozing off in the cave where I hid them, he reasoned. Which ones are real and which ones are unreal, he then started to ponder. While trying to trap Krishna in Maya, Brahma instead fell under its spell.

All these cowherd boys and animals that resembled Lord Vishnu at the same time. Finally, Krishna's spell was dispelled. Brahma immediately dismounted from his chariot, bowed to Krishna, and uttered the following words: "Salutations to Thee, O Lord. You are the One without a second, the Self, and the Indweller of all beings, as shown in the Brahma Purana.

No one is powerful than Him. He who killed several demons without any weapon, who danced on the hook of Kalaya Naag, who lifted Govardhan mountain from His small finger, is the most powerful. Krishna Himself says-

BG 10.41: Whatever you see as beautiful, glorious, or powerful, know it to spring from but a spark of my splendor.

Contradicting some modern age philosophers' opinions Lord Krishna says in BG 9.11 Fools deride Me when I descend in the human form. They do not know My transcendental nature and my supreme dominion over all that be. He is limitless so His powers are also limitless. But He use this power to save His devotees from all calamities.

Krishna brought the cowherd boys and the calves back to the banks of the Yamuna where they had been having a picnic exactly a year earlier after allowing Brahma to go on vacation. They felt as though only a moment had passed at that point. After finishing their feast with joy, they took Krishna back to their village and went home that night.

The Serpent Kaliya is Tamed

Following Brahma's permission to take a vacation, Krishna returned the cowherd boys and the calves to the Yamuna riverbanks where they had been enjoying a picnic exactly a year earlier. At that point, it seemed as though only a moment had elapsed. Joyously ending their feast, they returned with Krishna to their village and spent the night there. One day, unnoticed by his friends, Krishna climbed that Kadamba tree, and went out on the branches overhanging the river. Then he jumped into the river and swam fearlessly around.

The terrifying snake emerged from its hole in a rage after hearing water splashing. The snake encircled the lord. At that precise moment, terrible omens appeared in Vraja, which greatly alarmed the Gopas and Gopis. When they could not find Krishna anywhere, they desperately started looking for his footprints, which led them to the Yamuna where Kaliya was keeping him. While Krishna lay motionless in Kalaya's grasp, some of his young friends were found unresponsive on the riverbank.

The remaining Gopas and Gopis started crying out in adoration for their beloved Krishna. They believed he would undoubtedly be killed. Only Balarama was aware of his brother's strength; he counseled the others to exercise patience. While still being held by the snake, Krishna started to enlarge his body, which made the snake release him. He continued swimming around the snake until it was worn out. He then leaped onto the snakes' hoods and started to dance.

Devas from the heavens showered him with flowers after observing this beautiful scene. Krishna would step on it or dance around it whenever Kaliya attempted to raise one of his hoods. There were numerous mouths on the large snake, and blood began to erupt from each one. Finally, Kaliya started to consider the Lord, the Master of all creatures, and sought mental solace in him.

In the meantime, the wives of Kaliya hurriedly approached Krishna and humbly prayed, "O Lord! We do not know what admirable deed our husband did to earn the right to wear the dust of your feet on his head. Salutations to you, All-Indweller! We pray that you will accept us and spare our husband's life. Their prayer touched Krishna, who granted the snake's request.

Kaliya prayed to Krishna after he came to, saying, "Oord, please forgive me." We snakes are born with a bad disposition. One cannot change who they are by nature. This is only your own illusion. Do with me know what you deem appropriate.

Leave this location right away, and go to the sea with your wives, your family, and your friends, Krishna commanded. Krishna reassured the snake: "Now that you bear the marks of my feet on your head, Garuda will not harm you." Krishna was aware that Kaliya had fled the sea due to his fear of the enormous bird Garuda, who serves as Vishnu's carrier. After bowing to Krishna and giving him numerous gifts, Kaliya and his wives departed from the Yamuna to travel to the sea. Since then, the Yamuna River has been poison-free and has nectar-like sweetness to its waters.

Krishna Steals the Gopis' Clothes

It was a tradition of Vraj Culture; Gopis observe a month-long vow connected with the worship of Devi Katyayani. at the beginning of the winter season.

So, the young Gopi girls decided to observe this ritual. Getting up at sunrise, they would bathe in the river and then make offerings to the goddess. The purpose of this vow was to try to get Krishna as their husband.

Demigod worshippers occasionally mention that the Gopis worshiped Goddess Durga, but we need to know why they existed in the first place. Typically, people worship Goddess Durga to receive material blessings. The Gopis prayed to the goddess here to become Lord Krishna's wives. The implication is that if Krishna is the focal point of activity, a devotee can use any strategy to fulfill that objective. The Gopis were free to use any strategy to please or serve Krishna. That was the Gopis' fantastic quality. For a month, they offered their undivided worship to

Goddess Durga to win Krishna as their husband. They prayed for Krishna, Nanda Maharaja's son, to become their husband daily.

During this time, the Gopis regularly visited the river, hung their clothes on the bank, and bathed in the water. Krishna visited that spot by the river that morning as well after learning of their vow. Krishna gathered up all the Gopis' clothing without the Gopis' knowledge and climbed into a tree with them. From the top of the tree, he then called to the girls, saying, "I would like to help you all fulfill your vow. You can each come here and get your own cloth, then.

The Gopis were horrified by Krishna's remarks, and as they shivered in the river, they started to beg him to return their clothes, saying, "O Krishna, you know what you are doing is not proper." The Gopis eventually emerged from the river, covering themselves with their hands, after Krishna insisted that they must do so to get their clothes.

Lord Krishna was immediately pleased with them because of their humble presentation and because it was so pure. Thus, Katyayani was able to grant the wishes of all the single Gopis who had prayed to her for Krishna to be their husband. Except in front of her husband, a woman is not allowed to be exposed. The Gopis, who were not married, asked Krishna to be their husband, and He granted their request in this way. When He saw how happy they were, He took their clothes off them and said, "My dear girls, you have committed a great offense by going naked in the river Yamuna. Varuṇadeva, the dominant deity of the Yamuna, has grown angry with you as a result. To be excused, kindly touch your foreheads with your palms together and bow to the god Varuna.

All the Gopis were simple souls who believed whatever Krishna said to be true. They immediately followed Krishna's instructions to avoid Vasudeva's wrath, carry out the intended purpose of their vows, and ultimately please their worship able Lord. They developed into Krishna's greatest devotees and most obedient servants as a result.

Nothing compares to the Gopis' Krishna

consciousness. The Gopis was only interested in pleasing Krishna; they had no regard for Varuna or any other god. The Gopis' straightforward transactions won Krishna over, and He immediately sent each of them their matching garments, one by one. The young, unmarried Gopis was duped by Krishna, who made them stand naked in front of Him and laughed with them. He also stole their clothing and treated them like dolls, but despite all of this, the Gopis were still pleased with Krishna and never complained.

When Lord Chaitanya Mahaprabhu cries out in prayer, "My dear Lord Krishna, you may embrace Me or trample Me under Your feet, or You may make Me brokenhearted by never being present before Me," He is describing the attitude of the Gopis. You are completely free to carry out any action you please. Nevertheless, despite all Your dealings, I can only worship you because you are my Lord forever. This is how the Gopis feel about Krishna.

Krishna Blesses the Pious Brahmin Women

One day when Krishna and Balarama and the other Gopas had taken their cattle out to graze, they all became very tired and hungry. The boys said to Balarama and Krishna: 'We are overwhelmed with hunger. Do something to help us.'

Nearby there lived a group of brahmins who were then engaged in performing a long sacrifice. Krishna told the boys to go to these brahmins and beg for some food for all of them. The boys went, and after introducing themselves to the brahmins as messengers of Krishna and Balarama, they asked the men to give them some food. But the brahmins simply kept quiet and ignored the boys. They heard what the Gopas said, but pretended that they did not. At last, unable to get a response from them, the Gopas returned empty-handed to Krishna and told him what had happened.

Krishna then told the boys to approach the wives of those brahmin men, as he knew that they were pious and loved him very much. When the Gopas informed the women that Krishna was nearby and wanted some food, the women were thrilled. They immediately rushed to meet him, carrying all kinds of good food with them. Krishna also was happy to meet the women, who were sincerely devoted to him. After giving the food to Krishna, the women begged for refuge at his feet. They understood that from their actions their husbands and other family members would not accept them back in their homes. But Krishna assured them that they should have no fear. Through His grace, their families would accept them as if nothing had happened.

Before the women departed, Krishna told them to meditate on him and they would soon attain him thereby. Then Krishna, Balarama, and the other Gopas all began to eat. When the brahmin men returned to their homes and saw that their wives were so full of devotion to Krishna, they realized they had made a great mistake. They became extremely repentant and bitterly regretted their missed opportunity. Out of fear of Kamsa, they did not go to find Krishna, though they were anxious to do so.

A journey of a thousand miles begins with a single step and is sustained by a single step, as is rightly said. This idea can be applied to both a physical journey and our spiritual ascent of Krishna. If we just use the intelligence that God has given us, we can know that even when we can't see the entire path ahead, there is one thing we can always do: turn to Krishna in fervent prayer. We can take the one step of faith even on a dark road that will gradually move us towards illumination both internally and externally with such sincere prayerfulness, in addition to asking Krishna for guidance through his representatives.

When Arjuna, who is drowning in confusion, takes the one step that is obvious to him—turning to Krishna for guidance—the Bhagavad-Gita illustrates this pragmatic progressive application of faith (BG02.07). By the time Krishna has finished explaining the Gita's message, Arjuna is certain and certain about doing what Krishna wants (BG18.73). And throughout the Gita's narrative, Krishna reveals the maxim that can provide us with direction: If we try to serve Krishna in a loving and prayerful manner to the best of our ability, Krishna will give us the inner wisdom to continue drawing nearer to him (BG10.10)

Lifting Mount Govardhana

It has been believed the Indra is the rain god, people used to believe by worshiping Indra provides the clouds to give rain The rain nourishes all the crops, and refreshes the earth. Without rain it was impossible to think of living.

Nanda and the citizens of Vrindavan were preparing for a great sacrifice to Indra. Krishna then pleaded with Nanda: 'Please stop this worship. We are a race of cowherds. Our livelihood is not in plowing the land, but in looking after the cows. If we are to do any worship, we should worship the cows. Along with that, we should worship the brahmins, the poor, and this Govardhana hill. This hill is our home, and helps us so much. We can use these offerings that you have collected for Indra towards that worship.'

Everybody accepted the young boy's idea. From the items that had been collected, Nanda gave many gifts to holy men. Then he fed the poor sumptuously, gave plenty of good fodder mixed with oil cake to the cows, and worshipped Mount Govardhana. After

that, the cowherd folk circumambulated Mount
Govardhana. Krishna himself in one form assumed
the form of the mountain and ate large quantities of
the food. In another form, he remained with the
Gopas and Gopis and bow down before the
mountain.

Then they all returned to their homes. But Indra was
furious he did not like this action by the villagers. He
thought: 'These insignificant forest dwellers have
become very proud of their wealth. Depending on a
silly boy, they dare to ignore me!'

He then gave the order to the clouds: 'Crush their
pride! Submerge them with rain.' So, the clouds
descended on Vraja and deluged it with torrential rain.
The thunder roared, the lightning flashed, and the
rain fell and fell and fell. Vrindavan was about to be
washed away. At last, the Gopas and Gopis went to
Krishna and prayed to him to save him from the
wrath of Indra!'

Krishna then resolved to humble the pride of Indra.
Like a boy picking up a toadstool, Krishna picked up
Mount Govardhana with his left hand and called all

the people of Vraja to take shelter under it. Bringing all their belongings, along with their cows and calves, they stayed there safe from the raging storm. Krishna held Govardhana up with his left hand, like an umbrella, for one full week. He took neither food nor drink nor did he move an inch. Krishna lifting the Govardhana

Indra was stunned to see Krishna's power. He called the clouds back, and the rain stopped. Then Krishna also called all the people of Vraja to come out from underneath the mountain, and he put it back down where it had been before. All the Gopas and Gopis—and especially Yashoda, Nanda, Rohini, and Balarama—came and embraced him and pronounced benedictions over him. The devas also threw flowers on him and praised him.

Then Indra understood his mistakes and recognized the supreme lord and asked for forgiveness. Lord Krishna said, "I stopped the yajna to you to crush your pride of wealth and power. Those who are infatuated with wealth and power are unable to see me. So, when I wish to bestow my grace on someone, I first remove his wealth.'

Surabhi, the celestial cow, gave a consecration bath to Krishna with her milk. After that, Indra brought water down from the heavenly Ganga in vessels of gold, bathed Krishna with it, and consecrated him with the name Govinda.

KRISHNA HOLDING UP MOUNT GOVARDHANA.

Rasa Lila

An especially significant section of the Bhagavatam is the Rasa Lila. It is known as Rasapanchadhyaya because it was told in five chapters. Its focus is Krishna's dance with the Gopis on the Yamuna River's banks. This tale serves as an allegory for a very high level of devotion to God.

It was the full moon night in autumn. Moonlight-bathed Yamuna and her banks were breathtakingly beautiful. The moon floated in the sky like a lotus in full bloom. The Gopis were all occupied at home with their various responsibilities. Some were feeding their kids while others were milking their cows or making bread. They were startled to hear Krishna's flute playing entrancing melodies in the breeze.

Krishna had started to play as he stood on the Yamuna's bank, beaming with happiness. The Gopis' attention was immediately drawn to him. Whatever they were doing, they abandoned it and hurried to Yamuna's bank to see their beloved.

"Why have you come here at this hour?" Krishna asked the Gopis as they stood on the Yamuna's bank. After dark, vicious animals roam this area! Go home; it is not secure for you here. Where you have gone will be a mystery to your families. If you came to see the forest's beauty, then you have already seen it. Since all creatures are devoted to me, it is not surprising that you have come out of love for me. But you also need to take care of your husbands and families. You must do that. Please return home.

The harsh words of Govinda hurt the Gopis' hearts. "We have left our families and our wealth to worship at your feet," they declared. At those feet, we have found refuge. Do not leave us behind. You must accept us, just as God accepts everyone who seeks him alone. O Lord with lotus eyes, we cowherd women of Vraja yearn for your golden feet just as much as Lakshmi herself does. By touching your feet, we have already received blessings.

Later, Govinda gave his consent and started having fun with the Gopis by the Yamuna. But over time, the women's hearts started to grow proud. They started to believe that they were not typical people. We must be the most deserving women in the world for Krishna to pay us such lavish attention. Krishna vanished right away when this egotism crept into their hearts. He desired to make them pure. and make them deserving of his grace.

When Krishna vanished, the Gopis' suffering was beyond words. They started looking frantically and yelling, "O Krishna, where have you been? The longing drove them almost insane. "O Jasmine, O Mallika, have you seen where Krishna has gone," they questioned the forest flowers. Govinda is very fond of you, Tulsi. However, where is he? They yelled, "O Velva, O Kadamba, O all trees," to all the trees.

Krishna had become so dear to the Gopis that now, losing him, they were about to go crazy. Soon, their minds became so absorbed in the thought of Krishna that they even began to think that they themselves were Krishnas. They started acting as if they were Krishna. in various events in his Lila, like the killing of Putana and the taming of Kaliya, playing the flute, and the lifting of Mount Govardhana Like While roaming about the forest dazed, they suddenly came across a footprint of Krishna. How great was their joy just seeing his footprint! It was not difficult to recognize. In it, they could see the signs of Vishnu, the flag, lotus, thunderbolt, goad, and grain.

The Gopis returned to the location where they had first seen Krishna and sat down on the bank of the river, lost in thoughts of him. They prayed to him and frequently mentioned his many acts of kindness. "Just thinking of you brings us such joy," they said. The world's misery is banished by your words, which are like nectar to our ears. They who hear about you are blessed, and those who talk about you are truly blessed.

They are the greatest benefactors in the world. O Master, O Lord, it pains us to even consider that you might hurt your feet on the uneven ground and thorns of the forest. But oh! Where are you right now? You are everything to us; you are our life. We are hypnotized by the sounds of your flute and leave our husbands, kids, and all our other relatives to run to you. You simply need to present yourself to us.

The Gopis prayed in this manner and then sobbed uncontrollably. Krishna, the flute player dressed in a yellow robe, then materialized in front of them. They again lost their minds with happiness at that point. And it

At that point, Madanamohana, Hari, the god of love, started to interact with the Gopis more on the Yamuna River's bank. The bank of the river was covered in blooms. The sweet scent of the flowers drew honeybees, and they filled the air with their mellow hum. Krishna, the Gopis, the bank, the flowers, the trees, and the moon were all graciously illuminated by the moon's liquid silver light. Maybe if the splendor of the three worlds could unite for a single night to form one person, it would be as lovely as Krishna was that evening.

He stood out among the Gopis like the moon among the stars. Krishna then started the rasa dance. He multiplied himself using his yogic abilities, dancing between every two Gopis. Each Gopi noticed Krishna dancing next to her while holding her hand. They had been picturing Krishna and meditating on him the entire time. They now notice him standing next to them.

Krishna is both inside and outside. He is everything in the universe. Krishna, the Gopis, and God are all dancing right now. Krishna to the left, Krishna in the distance, Krishna to the right, and Krishna so nearby. There is no one else in the universe besides Krishna! Krishna, who is filled with bliss, resides in all beings, and gives each being always a taste of bliss. He is the epitome of happiness. This is how Gopis behave on the holy night of the rasa dance.

How Ajamila was Forgiven?

In ancient times, to become a perfect brahmana by studying the Vedas and following the rituals and regulative principles. Ajamila is one such brahmana. Ajamila was a very noble brahmin, performing his duties and prescribed rituals most sincerely and was also a good husband, good son, and good father.

Once when he was in the forest to gather the fuel-wood for his rituals, he fell for a woman, heart, and soul. The woman was one of very low morals. From that time onwards he lived with her, abandoned his family and his own parents. He had ten children by her, made a living and supported this large family by blackmailing rich people, by cheating, fraud, and gambling. He was particularly fond of the youngest child, Narayana, by name. The attachment to the child was so pronounced that whether he was eating, drinking, relaxing or working, he would always want Narayana to be by his side and partake of his food or participate in his enjoyment.

At the time of death Yamadutas came to take him to Yamaraja for punishment. In fear Ajamila loudly called the name Narayana because he was attached to his youngest son. Thus, he remembered the original Narayana, Lord Vishnu. Although Ajamila did not chant the holy name of Lord Narayana offensively, it acted nevertheless. Hearing the name of Narayana, the order carriers of Lord Vishnu immediately appeared. A discussion ensued between the order carriers of Lord Vishnu and those of Yama Raja. The Visnudutas said, "By changing the name of Lord Narayana once sufficiently atones for the sinful reactions of millions of lives." Chanting the glories of the Lord's holy name awakens all good fortune. When the Yamadutas were forbidden to take Jamila's soul, they went to their lord, Yamaraja, to tell him what had happened. They asked him who were the Visnudutas, how could they stop the order coming directly from Yamaraja? Yamaraja said, "My dear servants, you have accepted me as the Supreme, but factually I am not. Above me, and above all the other demigods, including Indra and Chandra, is the one supreme master and controller." He told them that the

Supreme Personality of the Godhead is fully independent and is the master of everyone. The Visnudutas, Vishnu's order carriers, protect the devotees of the Supreme Lord, even from the authority of Yamaraja. Having thoroughly understood the discussion between the Yamadutas and the Visnudutas, Ajamila became a pure devotee of Lord Narayana. Ajamila lamented and condemned himself. Because of his association with the Visnudutas, his original consciousness was aroused. Ajamila gave up everything and went to Haridwar, where he engaged in devotional service without deviation, always thinking of the Lord Narayana. At the end of Jamila's life, the Visnudutas went there, seated him on a golden throne, and took him to Vaikuntha.

That is the Lord Narayana., the Transcendental Absolute. It is his emissaries that take care of Dharma throughout the Universe. The greatest Dharma in the whole world is the recitation of His name. Even a one-time uttering of the name of God removes the person from my noose. It does not matter whether he takes the name intentionally or not.

Lord Krishna Himself emphatically says in the Bhagavat Gita. "He that has thought of Me alone, leaving his body comes forth to Me and enters my Being. Doubt this is not. But at the hour of Death, while laying off the body if one thinks of something else, he goes to what he looked for, because he has been in that mood all along. Therefore, Oh Arjuna, always, think of Me and fight Thou too, when your heart and mind are fixed on Me, shall surely come to Me."

Krishna's visit to Duryodhana and Vidura

Krishna will accept only offerings offered with love and affection. This was demonstrated by an occurrence in Hastinapur. Arjuna and his four brothers are well-recognized to be Krishna's children.

Duryodhana, who also lived in Hastinapur, Arjuna, and his brothers' sworn adversary (they subsequently battled each other at the Battle of Kurukshetra), yet he wished to invite Krishna to a feast.

Duryodhana was a wealthy man, so he offered delectable meals such as laddu, para, kachori, Sandesh, and Makhan on golden platters and water in golden cups.

"Come and share Your supper with Me," he said to Krishna. "I can't eat anything since I don't have an appetite," Krishna argued. I will never eat with you because you have no love and affection for me! I came to Hastinapur to request that you make peace with Arjuna and his brothers, but you have refused.

How can I bring my lunch to you? I'm neither a beggar, nor am I hungry."

Krishna went to Vidura's house shortly after refusing Duryodhana's lavish feast. Vidura was Krishna's devotee and was particularly fond of Arjuna and his four brothers. He had saved them from grave danger on countless occasions. Krishna adored Vidura because of this. When Krishna arrived at Vidura's house, Vidura was not present, so he begged his wife Vidurani Maiya, "Oh, Vidurani Maiya, I am so hungry!" Please provide me with something to eat." Vidurani had a strong attachment to Krishna and was eager to serve Him. She started to bring Him bananas, but in her perplexity, she threw the fruit away and only offered Him the peels.

Krishna embraced the peels with affection and delighted in them. These were sweeter to Him than all the preparations and offerings provided by his royal queens Rukmini and Satyabhama at Dwarka.

Vidura entered as Krishna was entirely interested in accepting Vidurani's donation of banana peels. He was taken aback by what he saw and shouted, "Oh, Vidurani! "What exactly are you doing?" Krishna tried to warn him, saying, "Don't speak to her. She is not in her physical body. She is completely consumed by spiritual love and affection." Vidurani, on the other hand, returned to external consciousness when she heard her husband talk and quickly comprehended what was going on.

She then gave Krishna the fruit of the bananas and threw away the peels. Krishna was a little disappointed. "Oh! This fruit is not as tasty as the peels were."

This activity demonstrates that Krishna is never hungry. He doesn't want to eat bananas, candy, milk, or anything else. He simply wishes to get the essence of all the fruits. What exactly is that essence?

It's simply love and affection—the bhakti attitude in the offering. Krishna will never take anything from someone who does not love and adore Him. He, on the other hand, would take what He wants from a devotee who loves and cares for Him if that devotee did not give Him enough.

Krishna is like that. Krishna is not a scrounger. He is opulent in every way, but He still comes to his believers and serves them.

In the Bhagavad Gita Krishna says: "Patram pushpam phalam toyam yo me bhaktya prayacchati, tad Aham bhakty-upahritam asnami prayatatmanah" If one offers Me with love and devotion a leaf, a flower, fruit, or water, I will accept it. So, in whatever we do, we should add bhakti, and our life will be perfect.

"Hare Krishna, Hare Krishna, Krishna Krishna, Hare Hare, Hare Rama, Hare Rama, Rama Rama, Hare Hare."

Story of Jada Bharata?

Before becoming Jada Bharata, Bharata was King Bharata, the oldest of Rishabh Deva's 100 sons and a powerful ruler who was also an incarnation of the divine. After several years of ruling, Rishabh Deva appointed Bharata as king and abandoned the world to become a traveling spiritual man. Bharata thereafter became King Bharata.

Bharata the Great was an excellent king. He had a deep love for the inhabitants of the kingdom and exercised loving control over them. He was such a successful monarch that India was given the name Bharat Varsha in his honor. He offered numerous sacrifices, and all their byproducts were given to Vasudeva, the Lord. As a result, his heart was cleansed, and he developed a strong commitment to the Lord.

After many years, he too had to leave the kingdom, much like his father, and spend the remainder of his days in prayer and meditation to God. Hence, he partitioned the realm among his five sons and moved into the Pulaha Ashrama, a remote ashrama. On the bank of the Gandaki River, Pulaha Ashrama was a stunning and revered location with woods on all sides. Several religious men saw the vision. King Bharata began his austere life of worship and meditation in that sacred setting.

While worshipping the Lord, meditating on him, and praying for his vision, tears would flow from his eyes out of longing and joy. His mind became fully fixed on the Lord.

During his morning devotion, Bharata would recite the holy word Om along the banks of the Gandaki river. A doe in pregnancy arrived at the river's edge to drink. The terrifying roar of a lion rang out of nowhere by way of the ashrama. The doe, shaken by fear, jumped to the other bank to escape. But her anxiety and effort were too great, and she gave birth to her child as she leaped. The tiny fawn subsequently fell into the river's swirling water. The mother doe passed away from shock in the interim. The royal sage witnessed everything that took place.

Bharata felt sympathy for the fawn without a mother. He carried it to the ashrama after saving it from the rushing floods. Bharata now began to care for the fawn without a mother. This poor fawn has no one to look after him, he thought to himself. Other than me, he has no one in this world. I must take care of him.

Bharata developed a deeper and deeper love for the fawn every day. He would gather grass and other food for him to eat, keep him safe from threatening creatures, and carry him around and pet him. Oh, where is my little deer? he would think if the fawn briefly disappeared from his line of sight. Bharata began to devote less time to worshiping Sri Hari and more time to thinking about and caring for his deer.

Gradually, Bharata lost all recollection of his adoration and meditation. He was thinking about the fawn and taking care of it nonstop. Fearful, Bharata would look everywhere for the fawn when it strayed off that it could have experienced something.

That small deer was the focus of his entire existence and way of thinking. King Bharata finally experienced the hour that must come to everyone: the moment of his demise. He lay still, watching his fawn resting by his side. He left his body while keeping the fawn front and center of his thoughts.

The thoughts that exist in a person's mind at the time of death determine what happens to them after death. King Bharata died while contemplating his deer, which caused him to soon reincarnate as a deer.

Bharata possessed a deer's body, but thanks to his meditation and devotion, he was still able to recall his previous life. Now he felt a great deal of regret. He lamented, "I was entirely devoted, but alas!"

I committed to God alone, focusing only on him when I somehow developed an attachment to a deer, leading to my birth as a deer. After leaving his deer mother, the deer Bharata traveled to the Gandaki River, which is close to Pulaha Ashrama. He stayed there alone while he awaited the day, he would be able to leave his deer body behind. Finally, Bharata was able to surrender his deer body to the river's waves.

Soon after, Bharata was reborn into a noble brahmin

family with enlightened and devout parents. Bharata was determined to avoid being discovered by the world this time. He pretended to be deaf to avoid people.

Although being stupid, dim, and of little intelligence, he was constantly thinking of Sri Hari. Others referred to him as Jada, inert because he appeared so foolish. His father tried to explain to him what a brahmin boy was, but it was useless. Jada Bharata refused to be instructed. He was left to fend for himself when his parents passed away and his brothers made a brief attempt to instruct him but failed. At times he even had to go without food because he had to work so hard at several jobs. Nonetheless, he was unaffected by any difficulties since he constantly felt the ecstasy of the Self within. Contemplating Sri Hari.

One day, King Rahugana was making his way to Kapila's ashrama in a palanquin. The captain of the palanquin carriers was looking for a substitute because one of the bearers was ill and unable to work.

He saw Jada Bharata, who was seated beneath a tree, urged him to replace the ailing carrier. The bearers grabbed Jada Bharata when he remained silent and put the palanquin's pole on his shoulder. However, despite being powerful, moved slowly and unevenly. To avoid stepping on any crawling insects or worms, he was watching the ground carefully.

The palanquin's uneven motion irritated King Rahughana, who questioned the captain about it. He was informed by the captain that the new bearer was not walking correctly. Jada Bharata was then teased by the monarch, who said, "Well, you must be so fatigued because you have been lugging this palanquin all by yourself." You have been so long with yourself. And you are a sickly old man!"

Jada Bharata continued to walk in the same manner despite the king's instructions. The monarch then grew enraged and yelled, "You fool! you still-alive corpse I'll make you into a corpse, as is your natural nature. I believe you require a good punishment. Jada Bharata opened his mouth at last and spoke for the first time in his life.

Who do you call a fool, O King? he asked. Who do you think is worn out? Whom do you address as "you"? If by "you" you mean this body, it is unconscious and formed of the same substances as your body. It cannot sense pain or fatigue because it is unconscious. Yet I am the Atman, the Soul, not this body. You refer to me as a dead body. It holds true for this body as well as all things with beginnings and ends. We are only temporarily the king and the servant.

There is no distinction between you and me other than convention. We both possess the Atman. O King, any thrashing would have no effect on me if I am acting oddly because I am grounded in the understanding of the Atman. Therefore, a beating would have no effect on me if I am a moron! Jada Bharata appeared to be an idiot, yet he had an endless supply of wisdom. Rahugana, the king, was a devout follower of God. He was astounded by Jada Bharata's comments and concluded that he must be a great saint after hearing them.

The King hastily exited the palanquin, knelt at the serene sage's feet, and asked him for forgiveness for what he had spoken. "Reverend Gentleman, I was unable to understand who you are," he said. You must be a wise person. I have a tremendous yearning for spiritual understanding after hearing what you said. Please treat me with courtesy. I lost my prejudice because of my sense of pride in being king. That is unquestionably a serious fault for me to have insulted a noble soul and a pious man. Save me from this sin, please. Please guide me in understanding the Atman, O intelligent one.

Then Jada Bharata started teaching the king and revealed his past, saying, "In a previous life, I was King Bharata. I spent my final days in thought and prayer, but in the end, I grew close to a deer whose life I had saved. I had a deer for the next life, but because of my life of prayer and devotion, I was able to recall my prior existence. In the body you see in front of you, I have now given birth once more. I stay away from people to prevent getting attached. The Absolute Lord is the ultimate Reality, and knowing

Him is the only purpose in life. You need the holy company of saints and sages to obtain this understanding. Our world is like a dark fog, a forest where people, roaming about looking for happiness, lose their way.

The five senses and their evil master, the perplexed intellect, make up the six horrible robbers in this woodland. They assault tourists and steal their belongings. They become caught in the creepers of worldly attachments as they wander around aimlessly in this forest, suffering from a variety of pains and afflictions. You are also in this jungle, O King. What exit is there? Love all living things, practice detachment, devote all your effort to the Lord, and, armed with the knowledge sword sharpened by Sri Hari worship, carve a path through the ignorance forest.

When you finally realize that you are the Atman and not the body, you will reach Sri Hari. The great sage Jada Bharata left to tour the country after advising King Rahugana. The monarch eventually gained Sri

Hari after realizing that he was the Atman and applying what he had been taught.

The Story of Markandeya

Shaunaka and the other sages at Naimisharanya were still curious about Shukadeva's speech to Parikshit even though it had already ended. They asked Suta to recount the extraordinary life of the sage Markandeya, who is thought to be eternal, for them.

Markandeya, the sage Mrikanda's son, began engaging in severe penances when he was a young child, according to Suta Mahamuni. He would recite the Vedas after worshiping Lord Hari each day, then gather a donation to his teacher. He would likewise eat from that food only if his teacher had given him permission. According to legend, he was able to defeat death because of his passionate adoration of the Lord. Over the course of his lengthy

He kept chastity and practiced austerities so that in meditation he might concentrate only on the Lord. In this way, he spent six manvantaras immersed in meditation.

Finally, out of fear that Markandeya might take over his position, Indra made the decision to send some apsaras, Gandharvas, and other creatures to distract the sage from his concentration. But their all attempts fell short. Indra was forced to concede defeat since Markandeya was unmoved at all. Moreover, Markandeya was not the least bit enraged by Indra's attempt to distract him from his meditation.

The Lord appeared to Markandeya in his twin form of Nara-Narayana to bestow a blessing after being delighted to observe Markandeya's complete devotion to him. Markandeya saw those two forms of Vishnu before him and fell at their feet and started to praise them with a hymn. The Lord then instructed him to request a boon because he was so moved by his great devotion. But what could a sage without desires want? His every ambition had been fulfilled by the Lord's vision. When Markandeya finally spoke, he declared, "I have a yearning to experience your maya, by whose power all the worlds and everyone who lives in them see duality in your non-dual being."

His request was granted, and the Lord smiled as he vanished. Because this sage asked to experience Maya, whereas everyone else prayed to be free from Maya. Markandeya then remained in his ashrama while he awaited the answer to his prayer. One day, a severe storm arrived. There was no break in the torrential downpour. It went on for days on end. The planet gradually became submerged in water as all the rivers, lakes, and oceans gradually exceeded their banks. Markandeya was still floating in the water. The entire globe was in pitch blackness, and everything and everyone else had been drowned. He floundered in the flood waters for what seemed like ages, hungry and thirsty, overtaken with sorrow and delusion.

After countless years, Markandeya at last noticed a small area of land elevated above the sea. The sage noticed an infant laying on a leaf in the center of the banyan tree that was there, on that island. The moment Markandeya laid eyes on the adorable infant with a dark green complexion sucking his toes, all her tiredness and sorrow vanished. Markandeya approached the infant to speak with him but hesitated. But as soon as he approached, the infant drew him into its mouth. Stranger still, inside the baby's stomach, Markandeya saw the entire universe as it had existed before the flood.

It was the same everywhere. Markandeya was extracted from the baby as it exhaled just as he was considering everything. Markandeya was once more submerged in the flood, but the baby's banyan tree was still there. Markandeya realized that the infant was Lord Vishnu, the subject of his meditation. When the infant gave him a lovely grin, Markandeya again walked up to embrace him. But the infant vanished in an instant, along with the banyan tree and the entire downpour. Markandeya returned to his ashrama the very next second, as if nothing had happened. Everything was the Lord's deception.

Later, Markandeya was found in meditation when Shiva and Uma visited the ashrama. When Markandeya opened his eyes, he was met by the divine couple and fell to his knees before them while praising them. Shiva commended Markandeya's devotion to Lord Hari and advised him to request a blessing because he was aware of Markandeya's suffering at the time of his encounter with the Lord's Maya. May I have an unwavering devotion to Sri Hari, to myself, and to all thy devotees, Markandeya answered. Then Shiva responded, "All of your requests have been granted, and in addition, your fame will endure eternally. Also, until the cosmic dissolution, you must lead a life of complete renunciation and illumination while being aware of the past, present, and future.

With devoted salutations to Lord Vasudeva, to Sukadeva, and with praise for the Bhagavata, Suta concluded this great Bhagavata Purana.

Story of Prithu Maharaj

King Vena, Prithu Maharaj's father, was a harsh and irreligious man. So, the great sages assassinated him in the interest of the populace. The great sages churned King Vena's body after his passing to produce a new King. King Vena's churning arms gave way to the appearance of Prithu Maharaj and Archi.

Afterward, Prithu Maharaj was given the title of King. As a King, Prithu Maharaj concluded that the lack of food grains was caused by mother earth. To punish her, he used a bow to follow the earth's cow-shaped contour. The earth, which was formed like a cow, gave up out of fear and prayed to Prithu Maharaj. She suggested to the King that he level the entire earth's surface. By ascending the hills with his bow and arrow, Prithu Maharaj thereby leveled all the rough areas on the surface of the planet. Prithu Maharaj then milked the earth to produce enough food for the populace. Afterward, King Prithu ordered the offering of 100 horses as sacrifices.

Indra stole the horse prepared for sacrifice during the

final horse sacrifice because he was envious of Prithu Maharaj. When Prithu Maharaj's son saw this, he was furious and pursued Indra to murder him. Prithu Maharaj's son did not shoot his arrows at Indra since he was falsely clothed as a sannyasin. Lord Brahma encouraged Prithu Maharaj to continue his sacrifice with just 89 more sacrifices. Lord Vishnu arrived on the scene after being satisfied with the offering. King Indra was watching as Lord Vishnu gave Prithu Maharaj instructions when he got ashamed of his own actions and knelt at Prithu Maharaj's feet. The King made homage to the Lord and then went back to his house.

The citizens had very tastefully ornamented their city when the King arrived. Prithu Maharaj increased his might after gaining personal support from Lord Vishnu. He substantially improved the land in this way. Once, King Pruthu ordered the assembly members to participate in a significant sacrifice and began the process. Following his speech, Prithu Maharaja was blessed by all the pious brahmanas, who praised him for his devotion to the Absolute

Personality of the Godhead. The four Kumaras, who was as brilliant as the sun, showed up at that point. The moment the King saw them, he bowed before them and began to worship them. Prithu Maharaj was taught about the Absolute Truth by the four Kumaras. Prithu Maharaj experienced terrible austerities in the forest after giving up family life. The King gradually attained complete freedom from all wants and steadfastness in his spiritual life. The King gave up his physical body because he was in Krishna consciousness. Afterward, Queen Arci constructed a flaming pyre, laid her husband's body on it, and stepped inside of its blaze. Prithu Maharaj and his wife Archi instantly obtained spiritual bodies after giving up their physical ones. Each of them was transported to the spiritual world on a stunning swan-shaped aircraft.

The Story of Prahlada Maharaj

The father of Prahlada Maharaj, Hiranyakashipu, desired immortality. Thus, he practiced a severe type of austerity and meditation. Hiranyakashipu appeased Lord Brahma and won the blessings he sought. Hiranyakashipu's wife, Kayadhu, was expecting a child at the time he was away carrying out austerities.

The demigods arrested her because they believed she was carrying another demon in her womb. Narada Muni stopped the demigods from taking her to the celestial planets and brought her to his ashrama instead. There, Kayadu received spiritual knowledge instruction from Narada Muni. Prahlada Maharaj took advantage of those directives while still in the womb by paying close attention. Prahlada Maharaj turns into a great follower of Lord Vishnu because of the advice given by Narada Muni.

Prahlada Maharaj preached to his schoolmates about Lord Vishnu when he was five years old. Hiranyakashipu threw Prahlada Maharaj from his lap after hearing him mention Lord Vishnu. Since

Prahlada Maharaj was a follower of Lord Vishnu, Hiranyakashipu made numerous attempts to have Prahlada killed. Big elephants trampled on Prahlada as they threw him to the ground.

When the Prahlada was not killed by the wild elephant, his father Hiranyakashipu imprisoned him in a room filled with deadly snakes. Because Prahlada completely surrendered to Lord Krishna, the snakes would not bite him. Prahlada was made to stand in hot oil. Prahlada was struck by the rakshasas with tridents. Prahlada sat in silence and meditated on Lord Krishna because he had complete faith in the Supreme Personality of the Godhead.

Prahlada was poisoned by the powerful demon Hiranyakashipu, who also subjected him to extreme cold, wind, and fire. However, because Prahlada was completely sinless, nothing could harm him. Prahlada was even thrown off a cliff, but the Supreme Personality of Godhead always kept him safe. Lord Narasimha Deva emerged from a pillar and engaged Hiranyakashipu in combat to save Prahlada Maharaj. Narasimha Deva used His nails to kill Hiranyakashipu to save Prahlada. The faithful Hiranyakashipu soldiers came to fight with Lord Narasimha Deva after Hiranyakashipu had been killed, but the Lord killed every one of them.

Lord Narasimha Deva remained enraged following the death of Hiranyakashipu, and all the gods were powerless to appease Him. Lord Brahma then requested Prahlada Maharaj to appease the Lord. Prahlada Maharaj's prayers had pleased Lord Narasimha Deva, who placed him on His lap. In the family of such a pure devotee, Lord Narasimha Deva assured Prahlada Maharaj, not only the devotee's father but also his ancestors for twenty-one generations are liberated. Lord Brahma and Shukracharya placed Prahlada Maharaj on the throne of the world after Lord Narsimha vanished.

Story of Vitrasena

King Chitraketu was Vritrasura's previous incarnation. When King Chitraketu's first wife, Kritadyuti, gave birth to a son, the child was later poisoned by Kritadyuti's cowives out of jealousy.

The King, who was crying, was then taught about the Supreme Lord by Narada Muni and Angira Rishi. King Citraketu then performed the congregational chanting of the Lord's glories while he was flying his aircraft and traveling through space.

King Chitraketu, who was traveling at the time, once saw Lord Shiva embracing Parvati while surrounded by a group of great sages. The King roared with laughter when he saw this. As a result, Mother Parvati cursed the King to turn into a demon in a fit of rage.

King Indra insulted Brihaspati, his spiritual leader, around the same time. King Indra lost all his wealth and was subdued by the demons because of his disrespectful behavior toward his spiritual leader.

Then King Indra and the other gods sought refuge with Lord Brahma.

Following Lord Brahma's orders, the demigods accepted the sage Visvarupa, as their priest. King Indra asked Visvarupa about Narayanakavaca. Indra beheaded Visvarupa because he secretly gave the demons the remaining yajna.

His father, Tvastha, offered a sacrifice to kill King Indra after Vishvarupa was slain. To increase Indra's enemies, Tvashta performed a fire sacrifice and chanted a mantra; however, because he mispronounced the mantra, the sacrifice gave birth to Vritrasura, who was Indra's enemy.

The demigods approached Dadhici Muni and begged for his body as instructed by Lord Vishnu. Dadhici's bones were prepared into a thunderbolt. Later, the demigods and the demons engaged in a fierce battle. This thunderbolt from Indra severed one of Vritrasura's arms. Vritrasura fought alongside Indra and taught the king about the Supreme Lord while using one arm. Later, Indra used his potent thunderbolt to cut off Vritrasura's head.

Everyone was happy when Vritrasura was killed, but King Indra wept because he knew he had killed the great Brahmana and devotee Vritrasura. Vritrasura (a brahmana) was killed by King Indra, and a personification of sin's reaction pursued him. King Indra spent a thousand years submerged in a lake inside the stem of a lotus out of fear of a personified sinful reaction.

Ambarisha and Durvasa

Lord Brahma appeared from Lord Vishnu's lotus-navel, according to the Shrimad Bhagavatam. And Marichi was born from Brahma's own thought. Vamana was the son of Kashyap, who was the son of Marichi. We just finished listening to Vamana's tale. Ambarisha, a supreme devotee, was born in this similar family.

Let's start by talking a little bit about Ambarisha's father, Nabhaga. Nabhaga was an excellent person. He spent many years studying at his guru's house, and when he came home, his brothers had already distributed the family's assets to one another. They gave their elderly father to him as Nabhaga share. When Nabhaga went to his father and told him this, his father said: 'You have been deceived by your brothers, for I am not some property to be enjoyed. But rest assured, my son. You will learn two mantras from me.

You must recite these two mantras when the nation's king holds a yajna. There are sages who do not know, and when they do, they will highly respect you. And indeed, that is what took place. The sages gave Nabhaga all the remaining wealth after the sacrifice because they were so pleased with him.

Rudra had a legal claim to that wealth because he was supposed to receive whatever was left over after a sacrifice. Rudra informed Nabhaga that all the wealth was legitimate when he arrived to collect it.

" The rishis have given it to me", Nabhaga retorted. Let your father resolve our disagreement, Rudra said. Let him choose who deserves to receive this wealth. After hearing all the information, Nabhaga father decided in favor of Rudra, and Nabhaga followed his instructions. He visited Rudra.

I handed everything over to him after apologizing humbly for stealing the wealth. This made Rudra very happy, and he returned everything to Nabhaga. Nabhaga had a good time all day. Kings envied him because of his wealth.

Ambarisha, his son, eventually received his father's property. Ambarisha, however, had no interest in wealth or property. His thoughts were focused on Sri Hari's lotus feet. Ambarisha used to spend most of his time in prayer and worship. His devotion was so intense that Sri Hari was very pleased with him and gave the order for his Sudarshan Chakra to watch over Ambarisha for the rest of his days. Ambarisha, who was by this point a king, was keeping the dvadashi vow one day. He completed the rituals associated with this vow after fasting for three nights in a row, and with the holy men in attendance blessing him, he was prepared to break his fast.

Durvasa, a renowned sage, suddenly appeared. Durvasa accepted Ambarisha's invitation to have lunch with him after being properly welcomed. Before giving the sage a meal, King Ambarisha was unable to break his fast.

However, Durvasa was taking his time because he had gone to the Yamuna to take a bath. Ambarisha's fast-breaking opportunity had passed when it was deemed lucky to do so. What should I do? asked the king. He kept his promise by taking a sip of water while thinking of Sri Hari, but he refrained from eating.

Ambarisha greeted Durvasa with respect when he emerged from his bath. However, Durvasa realized through his supernatural abilities that Ambarisha had broken his fast before making him an offer.

Durvasa lost control of his anger. He tore out one of his matted locks, and a vicious monster erupted from it and charged Ambarisha.

Ambarisha had no fear at all. He made no movement at all. He stood there and kept referring to himself as Sri Hari. Then, out of nowhere, the Sudarshan Chakra appeared and destroyed the monster. The Chakra then moved in the direction of Durvasa.

Durvasa jumped into motion. He sprinted to the far reaches of the planet, to every heavenly and subterranean region. The Sudarshan Chakra followed him everywhere. Out of desperation,

Durvasa asked Brahma for protection. I am unable to assist you, Brahma said. You have offended a Sri Hari devotee. Durvasa then fled to Kailash and sought refuge at Mahadeva's feet. Mahadeva told him there that he couldn't help either. Visit Vaikuntha. Only Sri

Hari has the power to save you. Durvasa fled to Vaikuntha and sought refuge with Sri Hari, the city's king.

Sri Hari declared, "I am not free; I am subject to my devotee. How can I desert those who come to me and find solace in me alone? My heart belongs to true devotees, and I am the heart of the devotees. I know no one besides them, and they know no one besides me. "Learning and austerities are of immense good for spiritual aspirants," continued Sri Hari. However, for the haughty and conceited who use them.

They can be very harmful if they learn to try to hurt others. So, visit Ambarisha, the great devotee you feel you have wronged. pleading for his pardon. Only then will your error be absolved. Durvasa went to Ambarisha as directed by Sri Vishnu, knelt at his feet, and begged for forgiveness. The king felt extremely embarrassed that the rishi was clutching his feet. He then began to sing the praises of the Sudarshan Chakra.

"O Sudarshan!" he prayed. You are the defender of the Dharma and the asuras' greatest fear!

The entire world is under your protection, you! Be gracious and pardon this holy man's transgression. As a result, the Sudarshan Chakra was calmed, saving Durvasa. "O King, today I have seen the wonderful greatness of the servants of God," Durvasa said to King Ambarisha. while I despite having hurt you, have helped me. You really do have a lot of compassion. You have been a blessing to me. You have forgiven my transgression and preserved my life.

King Ambarisha had not eaten anything during this entire time. He was patiently awaiting Durvasa. The king then served the sage a lavish feast to his satisfaction, and Ambarisha, at last, began to eat.

Who is Maharaja Parikshit?

Parikshit Maharaj was the son of Abhimanyu and grandson of Arjuna in the Mahabharata. King Parikshit was in the womb of Uttara when the Kurukshetra war ended and he was the only remaining heir in the family of the Pandavas.

After 24 years as the ruler of Hastinapur, Parikshit retired to the forest and eventually perished due to a curse; Janamejay took over. He was given the Shrimad Bhagavatam by Sukadeva Goswami at this time since he was under a curse and would otherwise pass away in seven days.

Uttara, the mother of Parikshit Maharaj, hurried near Lord Krishna as he was getting ready to leave Hastinapur following the battle of Kurukshetra out of concern for the Brahmastra Ashwatthama had let loose. Lord Krishna wrapped the Uttara embryo with His own energy in order to safeguard the Kuru dynasty's future descendants. Yudhishthira Maharaj installed Parikshit Maharaj as the earth's ruler after

Lord Krishna vanished from the physical realm and retired to the forest.

Parikshit Maharaj, the world's monarch, was a strong leader who even reprimanded Kali. Parikshit Maharaj once grew so exhausted, hungry, and thirsty while hunting. He went into Shamika Rishi's hermitage in search of a water source. When Parikshit Maharaj was not given a proper greeting, he angrily picked up a dead snake and threw it on the sage's shoulder. The Rishi's son cursed Parikshit Maharaj to pass away in seven days after learning of his father's plight. When Parikshit Maharaj learned about the curse, he went to the wilderness to fast until he died, accepted Sukhdev Goswami as his spiritual guru, and submissively enquired of him. Parikshit Maharaj received the Shrimad Bhagavatam from Sukhdev Goswami. Parikshit Maharaj attained perfection by hearing the Shrimad Bhagavatam. After hearing the Shrimad Bhagavatam, Parikshit Maharaj passed away while meditating on Lord Krishna.

Rantideva

Despite descended from King Bharata, Rantideva lived a hermit lifestyle with his family. Even though he had nothing, whenever he saw someone in need, he would work to make things better.

Despite their suffering, he saw the Lord in all living things. He once encountered a situation where he was unable to obtain food for 48 days. The family was suffering from severe hunger and thirst. Finally, Rantideva was successful in getting some rice pudding with ghee, wheat, and water by begging. The sight of the food brought great relief to his family.

Just as Rantideva and his family were about to begin eating, a brahmin visitor showed up. Rantideva very kindly served food to the visitor after observing Lord Hari residing within him, and the brahmin left.

Following this, Rantideva divided the remaining food among the family members and was about to sit down to eat when another visitor—a laborer— arrived. seeing the Lord once more. The food that

Rantideva had just finished dividing for himself and his family was given to him by the guest who was living within him. The guest ate it and then departed.

Unexpectedly, a hunter with several dogs joined the party. He begged Rantideva, saying, "I'm starving." My dogs are, too. Give us something to eat, please. Only a few food scraps remained, which Rantideva shared with the visitor and his dogs. He then gave them a salute after recognizing Sri Hari in them. Then, there was absolutely no food left for Rantideva. There was hardly any water left. Just as he was about to sip that, a pariah barged in and begged for something a minimum of some water.

"I do not ask God for the eight miraculous powers," Rantideva assured him. I don't even supplicate for my own release. All I want is to live among all beings and experience their sufferings. They will be relieved of their misery by my taking on their sufferings. I have been freed from all sufferings—hunger, thirst, exhaustion, physical ailment, sorrow, and mental confusion—by giving the life-giving water to a man panting for it in great distress.

The suffering outcaste was then given whatever water was available by Rantideva. Rantideva had been put to the test by Brahma, Vishnu, and Shiva the entire time. They were the ones who arrived as the brahmin, the outcast, the laborer, and the hunter with the dogs. They now presented their true selves to Rantideva.

Despite his difficult situation, Rantideva bowed to them but refused to ask for any favors because he had no desire for anything. He had completely given himself over to Lord Vasudeva. All those yogis who followed Rantidev's example and became close friends with him attained complete devotion to Lord Narayana.

Yayati and Devayani

Devayani, the Asuras' spiritual leader Shukracharya's daughter, and King Vrishaparva's daughter Sharmishtha were close friends. They went to a park one day and relished taking a dip in the lake.

However, Princess Sharmishtha unintentionally donned Devyani's dress. Devayani insulted the princess because she was so offended. "Like a dog eating up the offerings meant for a yajna," she remarked. Sharmishtha was unwilling to accept such behavior with strong language. It is true, she reasoned, that I erroneously wore However, that does not give Devayani the right to mistreat me.

Sharmishtha got very angry, pushed Devayani into a well after insulting her and her father, and then went back to the palace. At that time King Yayati was hunting in that park. He happened to come close to the well in which Devayani was trapped and heard her wails. He rushed to the helpless girl's rescue and pulled her out of the well. Gradually they became enchanted with each other, and Yayati promised to marry Devayani. He then took leave of her. When Devayani went to her father and told him what Sharmishtha had said and done, Shukracharya was disheartened and decided they should leave the kingdom.

But when King Vrishaparva's heard about it he approached the preceptor, knelt at his feet, and begged for his pardon. The I can forgive you, but you must carry out the instructions of the demon guru.

Devayani.' As soon as my father gives me the okay, wherever I go, Devayani said. Sharmishtha will need to join me in marriage as me along with her attendants, a maidservant. King Vrishaparva's at the time. Worried about the consequences of Shankaracharya's departure for his kingdom, he agreed.

According to Devyani's wish, Shukracharya married her to King Yayati, and as per the agreement with King Vrishaparva's, Sharmishtha accompanied her to her husband's place as her maidservant. Before they left, Shukracharya commanded Yayati, 'You must never share a bed with Sharmishtha.'

Devayani eventually gave birth to a boy. Sharmishtha begged King Yayati to grant her wish because she was denied the pleasure of having a child. Shukracharya had forbidden Yayati from interacting in any way with Sharmishtha, but destiny had other plans. The king was under pressure to grant Sarmistha's wish. Sharmishtha gave birth to three sons over the years.

When Devayani eventually discovered that Sharmishtha had offspring with Yayati, she erupted in rage. She divorced her husband and went back to live with her father. However, Yayati fell deeply in love with Devayani and started pursuing her. He pondered, "How can I survive without her?" As they were leaving, he pleaded with her earnestly to stay, but he was unsuccessful. Finally, they both showed up at the home of Shukracharya.

Shukracharya had concerns about this. He scolded his son-in-law, calling him an "unfaithful creature," and expressed his deep distress at the turn of events. You disobeyed my command! You will become a sluggish old man and lose your youthful vigor! If any young man is willing to accept your old age, then you may exchange your old age for his youth, Shukracharya modified his curse after King Yayati begged for his pardon.

As a result, King Yayati grew old and frail, but he continued to yearn for sensual experiences. He then asked his oldest son, Yadu, to accept his advanced age. But what typical individual would forgo worldly pleasures before first relishing them? Yadu argued against it. Then Yayati asked each of his other sons, but they all declined to do so. Finally, he questioned his eldest son: Puru.

Puru said, "I am truly fortunate to have this once-in-a-lifetime opportunity to adequately compensate my father, who gave birth to my body. I will obtain the greatest good by making him happy. As a result, Puru accepted his father's advanced age, while Yayati benefited from the full vitality of his son's youth. Yayati relished the pleasures of life to his heart's content for a thousand years with his restored youth.

However, his need for amusement persisted. As a matter of fact, it was rising daily. Yayati's wife Devayani overheard him say, "Being duped by maya, I have forgotten what is good and what is bad," as his realization finally hit him.

Pouring ghee onto a fire does not put it out; rather, the fire leaps higher and higher. The fire of desire is also never quenched by pleasure. Pleasure only fuels desire. Therefore, if one truly desires the best outcome for themselves, one should give up their desire for enjoyment without hesitation.

Then Yayati gave his son Puru back his youth along with the entire kingdom. He accepted his old age, and immediately left for a forest to practice meditation on God.

Devayani dedicated her mind to Sri Krishna after realizing that this world is nothing more than the Lord's illusion. She made a mental bow to him and uttered, "O Lord Vasudeva, I salute Thee." You are the Supreme Person who resides in every living thing. I submit to You.

Dushyanta and Shakuntala

A very powerful king by the name of Dushyanta once ruled the Kuru dynasty, the family into which Parikshit was born. He went hunting one day with some of his men, and they eventually arrived at the Kanva the sage's hermitage. He came across a stunningly beautiful girl in this hermitage. Her beauty illuminated the entire hermitage.

Instantly falling in love with her, Dushyanta started conversing with her. Who are you, O lotus-eyed beauty? he questioned. You are whose daughter? And why are you in this forest right now? You can't be the hermit's daughter; you must be some kings!

I am the daughter of Vishwamitra and Menaka, who left me in the forest, Shakuntala retorted. Kanva has raised me with love and consideration. Shakuntala is my name. Stunning one! Take a seat, please. If you'd like, you can stay here.

"O beautiful one, the daughters of kings have the right to choose their own husbands," Dushyanta then remarked. It's known as a Gandharva marriage.

Dushyanta and Shakuntala were wed there and then after Shakuntala gave her consent to the union.

Dushyanta went back to his capital the following day. Shakuntala eventually gave birth to a son, whom she named Bharata. The sage Kanva provided the boy with tender care as he grew up. The young prince gradually got stronger to the point where he could play with and even catch lions.

Prince Bharata was taken by Shakuntala to her husband Dushyanta's palace after a while. Dushyanta, however, refused to accept Bharata as his son or Shakuntala as his wife.

Then, a voice from above was audible, proclaiming, "O Dushyanta, Bharata is truly your son." In him, a portion of your soul has been born. Accept your son, and spare Shakuntala any humiliation.

King Dushyanta immediately accepted his wife and son after realizing his error. Bharata succeeded to the throne of this Bharat Varsha following the death of Dushyanta.

Shakuntala's story is one of both tragedy and hope.
Abandoned in the forest by her own mother, she was
fortunate enough to be protected by a bird named
Shakunta. It was this bird that gave her the name that
she would carry with her for the rest of her life. But
fate had more in store for Shakuntala, as she was
discovered by Kanva Rishi, who took her under his
wing and brought her to his ashram. It was there that
she received the love and care that every child
deserves, and it was there that Kanva Rishi became
her father in every sense of the word. For Shakuntala,
the concept of fatherhood was not limited to
biological ties, but extended to those who provided
love, guidance, and support throughout her life. And
though her early years were marked by hardship and
abandonment, Shakuntala's story is ultimately one of
resilience and triumph over adversity.

Usha and Aniruddha

The King Bali tale has already been told. Sonita Pura's ruler was Bana, King Bali's son. Bana was blessed by Lord Shiva with a thousand arms because of which he became extremely strong.

One day Usha, his daughter, had a dream about an incredibly attractive young man. For this prince who had appeared in her dream, the princess nearly lost her mind. Chitralekha, the prime minister's daughter, noticed Usha's state and inquired, "My dear friend, what's wrong with you?" Why do you seem so upset? Tell me everything, please.

Usha retorted: In a dream, I saw a very attractive man standing in front of me. This man is the most handsome I've ever seen. Yet alas! I'm not familiar with him. Chitralekha had no trouble solving this issue. She was endowed with a remarkable talent for drawing portraits of all the kings and princes. Chitralekha uses this extraordinary ability of hers and kept on drawing pictures of kings and princes one after another. When Chitralekha finally created a drawing of Aniruddha, the grandson of Usha, who is the daughter of Pradyumna, looked down shyly and declared, "He is the one."

Chitralekha possessed yet another yogic ability. She had the ability to fly anywhere she desired. She flew to Dwarka, where she picked up the photo of Aniruddha, Krishna's grandson, after realizing that it was of him. Taking the sleeping prince from his bed, Usha at Shonitapura received him. Usha was ecstatic to finally meet the man she had been dreaming of, and Aniruddha was mesmerized by Usha's elegance and beauty. He lived covertly in Usha's apartment still.

However, such information could not be kept a secret for long, and the king soon learned of it. One day, he and some soldiers went to his daughter's apartment to see for themselves. When they arrived, they discovered Aniruddha and Usha playing dice. Bana was enraged. When the prince saw the soldiers enter with Bana, he grabbed a mace and started beating them. However, the potent Naga pasha (serpent noose) of King Bana soon imprisoned him.

Narada, a wise man, then went to tell Krishna. Your grandson Aniruddha is being held hostage in King Bana's palace in Sonitapura, he said. When Krishna learned this, he immediately led his army to the kingdom of Bana the Great. There was a bloody conflict. Shiva, who was standing there on Bana's side, was defeated by Krishna with the aid of a weapon that put Shiva to sleep. King Bana took up arms against Krishna after many of his warriors were decimated, and he continued to shoot thousands of arrows at Krishna with his thousand hands. But Krishna could not be easily frightened. He retaliated by using his potent Sudarshan Chakra. He continued to chop off one arm with the Chakra's assistance after another of King Bana till the king was left with only four arms.

King Bana's strength came from Shiva's boon, which is why Mahadev helped him. He begged Krishna, saying, "Bana is one of my greatest devotees. In addition, he is a progenitor of Prahlada, who has received your blessing. I beg you to pardon him and have mercy on him.

Prahlada and his descendant King Bali are devoted to me, Krishna retorted. I had vowed to Bali that I wouldn't murder any of his family members. I am therefore unable to murder Bana. But I'm here to make him humble. He will be able to rule his kingdom with the four remaining arms. I have destroyed his army so that the weight of the earth is lessened. I can assure Bana that he won't be put to death. King Bana bowed before Krishna's lotus feet in a gesture of gratitude.

Thus, the roadblock to Usha and Aniruddha's marriage was removed. Usha, the daughter of King Bana, was given to Aniruddha. Then, returning to Dwarka in his golden chariot together with his bride and his grandson.

The Last Advice of Sri Krishna to Uddhava

The sixth through the twenty-ninth chapters of the Shrimad Bhagavatam's eleventh Skandha is very significant. The Uddhava Gita, which consists of these chapters, is a collection of Krishna's final instructions to Uddhava.

Then, Uddhava prayed,

1. "O Lord, please explain to me how a person might achieve liberty while engaging in deeds motivated by the three gunas. What distinguishes a free spirit from a bound soul? How does a soul that is free act? How then can the soul, which is unbound and eternally free, be bound?

Though the Self, or soul, is always free and pure, Krishna retorted, it appears to be in servitude when it is connected to the three gunas. But because my own maya might create the gunas, the Self in fact is never constrained. As a soul experiences a variety of things when in the dream state, so too does it, while being fooled by my Maya, experiencing happiness and suffering, pain and pleasure, and birth and death. Nevertheless, they never meet the Self, the Atman within. Know, O Uddhava, that my Maya has two aspects: vidya maya, which dissolves delusion and causes the soul to recognize its connection to and oneness with me, and avidya maya, which causes the soul to believe it is an actual physical being. Let us take an example.

"Two lovely birds with identical plumage, who are pals, have made their nests on the same tree. One of them, the imprisoned soul, continuously consumes the tree's sweet and sour fruit. The other bird, known as the free soul, never consumes food, yet it is always robust and magnificent. The wise soul always revels in the knowledge of his own wonderful nature as Satchidananda, remaining forever detached from the good and terrible deeds of this world (Absolute Existence, Absolute Consciousness, and Absolute Bliss). But, the bound soul, fooled by this world, is unaware of his true nature and repeatedly experiences both birth and death.

2. "Oh Krishna, you truly are that supreme
    Brahman, without beginning or end," said
    Uddhava. Within you, the entire cosmos
    exists. You created the universe, and you once
    more reside within everything. But despite
    their Maya-induced delusion, people fail to see
    you. Please explain to me where and how you
    manifest yourself most.

Arjuna posed a similar query to me just prior to the
Battle of Kurukshetra, according to Krishna. I shall
tell you in brief what I told him. "I am the King of all,
the Self of all, and their friend. I create all entities out
of myself; I maintain them, and then they all return to
me. All entities live and move because of my might. I
am "Om" among all mantras. I am the Gayatri in
meters. I am Indra, the deva. I am among the eight
Vasus is Agni (Fire). I am the Vishnu among the
Adityas. I am Bhrigu among the great sages. I am
Manu, one of the royal sages. I am Narada among the
celestial sages. I am Kapila, one of the accomplished
yogis. I am Garuda, one of the birds. I am Prahlada in

the Demon dynasty. I am the moon among the planets. I am Kubera in the kingdom of Yakshas and Rakshasas.

I am Airavata, the elephants' leader. In terms of people, I am a king. In the equine world, I am Uchchaishravas. Of all the metals, I am the gold. I am the Ganga, the most holy of the rivers. I am in the Himalayas among the outlying regions. I am the Ashwattha in the tree world (peepul). I make a vow of non-violence. I am in the season of spring. I am Margashirsha, one of the months from December to January.

Among the four Yugas, I am the Satya Yuga. I am Vasudeva among people who are referred to as Bhagavan; among followers, I am you (Uddhava). I am Hanuman among the Kimpurushas and Sudarshan among the Vidyadhara. Among the offerings' materials, I am the cow's ghee. I am the riches of the diligent. I am the power that enables the powerful. I am the hero, Arjuna. I am each of the five elements: fire, earth, space, and the air. I am Purusha and Prakriti, as well as the ego, cosmic intellect, and all variations of Prakriti. I am rajas, tamas, and sattva. I am each of these and the highest Brahman. The only thing that exists is myself. Manage your voice, your intellect, your vital power, and your senses, Krishna continued to advise Uddhava. Control your lower self by your higher self. If this is achieved, one becomes free from samsara (the world).'

3. How are Yama and niyama described, O Krishna?

"Non-violence, honesty, non-covetousness, detachment, humility, non-accumulation of money, faith in the guru and the scriptures, chastity, moderation in speech, patience, forgiveness," says Krishna. These twelve qualities are Yama. These twelve practices are referred to as niyama: maintaining physical and mental purity, reciting the Lord's name, austerity, sacrifice, self-belief, hospitality, worship, traveling on pilgrimage, working for other people's well-being, contentment, and service to one's teacher. Those who engage in these disciplines "achieve the highest."

4. What constitutes genuine delight and genuine grief, asks Uddhava? Who is knowledgeable and who is uninformed? What are the meanings of heaven and hell? Which friend is this? What separates the wealthy from the poor?

Krishna: "Being unaffected by both pleasure and grief is the definition of true satisfaction. The root of genuine grief is attachment to sensual pleasures. Someone who can distinguish between slavery and freedom is intelligent. The body and its sensory organs are everything to such an uneducated person. When sattva rules the mind, it is in heaven; when tamas rules it, it is in hell. The only person who is a true friend is the guru. One who possesses all the virtues is affluent; meanwhile, one who is never content with anything is impoverished.

5. "O Krishna, I believe the path of yoga you have described is quite challenging. Please describe a straightforward approach for someone like me to achieve emancipation.

The Lord speaks. I will now explain the devotional path that can deliver someone from the abyss of death.

"When you perform your duties, constantly keep me in mind and submit to me. Maintain association with the holy and follow their example. You should celebrate the holy days to respect me. You will recognize me in every living thing once such observations have cleansed your mind. One who sees the good and the bad, the holy and the evil, the sun and a spark of fire, everything as aspects of me, genuinely illuminated, is that individual. The best way to find me is to see me in all beings. To surrender all one's actions at the feet of God is the surest way to attain liberation.

"I have explained to you the main points of the Vedas' teachings about Brahman. All your skepticism will go away after hearing these lessons, and you'll achieve liberation. a person with whom I share these teachings out of love for them. Yet trying to convince the arrogant atheists of this truth will be fruitless. Have you, Uddhava, been able to fully understand this ultimate instruction on Brahman? Do you no longer experience sorrow or delusion?

Uddhava bowed before Krishna's lotus feet and cried, "O Immortal One, O primeval Lord!" Thanks to your unending charity for me, my hallucination has disappeared today. You were the one who first tied me with your love, which was communicated through your Maya, and you were the one who again broke this bond with the sword of wisdom. I humbly submit to you, the greatest of all yogis. I have sought safety with you. May my thoughts constantly remain on your lotus feet. May my love for you never weaken or change. In addition, Krishna advised him to visit his residence at Badrikashrama. There, you should give everything I've said to your serious thought and focus entirely on me. By doing so this supreme dharma, you will gradually be freed from this relative existence and will attain my Supreme State.'

Both the Bhagavat Gita and Uddhava Gita are significant scriptures in Hinduism. While the former is focused on the conversation between Krishna and Arjuna during the Kurukshetra war, the latter is a discourse given by Krishna to his friend Uddhava before his departure from Earth. The Bhagavat Gita is a part of the epic Mahabharata, while the Uddhava Gita is a part of Shrimad Bhagavatam, both written by sage Vyasa. Both these texts offer valuable insights into spirituality and provide guidance on how to lead a fulfilling life. Despite their differences, both scriptures share common themes such as devotion, self-realization, and detachment from material desires. These texts continue to inspire millions of people around the world and serve as a source of spiritual wisdom for generations to come.

Author's Note

The Shrimad Bhagavatam is also known as Bhagavata Purana has for centuries been one of the favorite religious texts of India, and this is mostly because of its charming and attractive stories. For those people whose busy schedule does not allow them time to go through the complete Purana, I have brought out this collection of stories from the Bhagavatam. Every story has a life lesson. One can relate it to their own life.

Here readers will find all their favorite stories—the story of Prahlada, of Dhruva, of King Bharata, and many more. There are stories of rishis, kings, heroes, avatars, and of devas and asuras. But along with the stories, the Bhagavatam also presents relevant teachings. The content is written in plain and simple English without the Sanskrit verses, so that everybody can understand and relate to the stories.

What the Bhagavatam is most known for, however, are the stories of Krishna's life, from his birth in a dungeon in Mathura to his passing away at Prabhas.

Almost all his stories are included in this volume his childhood in Vrindavan, his youth in Mathura, and his later years in Dwarka.

To keep the volume to a reasonable length, the topics are divided into stories, characters, and philosophical approaches from the start to the end. I have had to condense these accounts. This is my sincere approach to making the text as simpler as possible. However, the main points of the stories are contained here. This volume is especially helpful for readers who do not yet know the stories and would like to learn them. But it is also helpful for readers who know the stories already—or at least some of them—as this volume will refresh their memories and help them learn many new stories. And, above all, it is an invaluable reference for children. May the ageless stories contained in this book fill the minds of its readers with devotion to the Supreme Being.

About The Author

The author is an Indian-Canadian who was born in the Indian Subcontinent state, of Odisha.

In a world where consumerism is rampant and the pursuit of material possessions is often equated with success, it can be difficult to find contentment and happiness. The author's desire to write more books that address these issues is commendable, as it speaks to a need for guidance in navigating the complexities of modern life. By offering practical advice and sharing personal experiences, the author can help readers find fulfillment beyond material possessions. It is important to remember that true success and happiness come from within, rather than from external factors such as wealth or status. Through thoughtful reflection and intentional action, readers can learn to prioritize what truly matters in life and cultivate a sense of purpose and meaning.

Mr. Das, possesses more than 25 years of professional work experience in the fields of education and technology in India, the United States, and Canada.

He is highly passionate about spirituality, philosophy, and ancient Indian texts. Mr. Das holds university degrees in Management and Physics. He enjoys conducting research, writing, presenting, and inspiring youth about the laws of nature, attractions, etc. Spirituality & Leadership, Youth Mentoring, Women Empowerment. Educational Technology, Educational Philosophy, Technology Integration into Education, Understanding of Self, and Teachings of Ancient Scriptures of India, and, Science & Spirituality are among a few of his favorite discussions.

So, if you are looking for a comprehensive guide to the wisdom of India, look no further than Mr. Sunil Das K's groundbreaking publication! Ultimately, the author's goal is to help readers deal with materialistic problems and inspire them to live their best lives by embracing what truly matters.

He is a devoted follower of Lord Krishna and the teachings found in the Bhagavad Gita and Shrimad Bhagavatam, among other ancient texts.

His approach is unique and refreshing, as he blends is

deep knowledge of the subject matter with a clear and concise writing style. The book covers a wide range of topics, from the history of India to the teachings of ancient sages. It also includes practical advice on how to apply these teachings to modern life. Mr. Das has done an excellent job of making these complex ideas accessible to a wider audience, without sacrificing any of their depth or richness. Whether you are a seasoned scholar or a curious beginner, this book is sure to provide valuable insights and inspiration.

References

Prabhupada, A. C. (n.d.). *Krsna: The Supreme Personality of Godhead.* Bhakti Bedanta Book Trust.

Prabhupada, H. D. (n.d.). *Bhagavad-gita As It Is.* Bhakti Bedanta Book Trust.

Prabhupada, H. D. (n.d.). *Śrīmad-Bhāgavatam.* Bhakti Bedanta Book Trust.

THE ESSENCE

Made in the USA
Columbia, SC
19 July 2023

20421153R00111